UNLOCKING
THE BIBLE

NEW TESTAMENT BOOK III

Through Suffering to Glory

UNLOCKING THE BIBLE

NEW TESTAMENT BOOK III

Through Suffering to Glory

David Pawson

with Andy Peck

Marshall Pickering
An Imprint of HarperCollins*Publishers*

Marshall Pickering is an imprint of
HarperCollins*Religious*
Part of HarperCollins*Publishers*
77–85 Fulham Palace Road, London W6 8JB

First published in Great Britain in 2001
by HarperCollins*Religious*

1 3 5 7 9 10 8 6 4 2

The chapter on Revelation was previously
published in *When Jesus Returns*
(Hodder & Stoughton, 1995)
and is published by kind permission of
Hodder & Stoughton

A catalogue record for this book is
available from the British Library

ISBN 0 551 03193 X

Printed and bound in Great Britain by
Omnia Books Limited, Glasgow

CONTENTS

INTRODUCTION

I suppose this all started in Arabia in 1957. I was then a chaplain in the Royal Air Force, looking after the spiritual welfare of all those who were not C.E. (Church of England) or R.C. (Roman Catholic) but O.D. (other denominations – Methodist to Salvationist, Buddhist to atheist). I was responsible for a string of stations from the Red Sea to the Persian Gulf. In most there was not even a congregation to call a 'church', never mind a building.

In civilian life I had been a Methodist minister working anywhere from the Shetland Islands to the Thames Valley. In that denomination it was only necessary to prepare a few sermons each quarter, which were hawked around a 'circuit' of chapels. Mine had mostly been of the 'text' type (talking about a single verse) or the 'topic' type (talking about a single subject with many verses from all over the Bible). In both I was as guilty as any of taking texts out of context before I realized that chapter and verse numbers were neither inspired nor intended by God and had done immense damage to Scripture, not least by changing the meaning of 'text' from a whole book to a single sentence. The Bible had become a compendium of 'proof-texts', picked out at will and used to support almost anything a preacher wanted to say.

With a pocketful of sermons based on this questionable technique, I found myself in uniform, facing very different congregations – all male instead of the lifeboat-style gatherings I had been used to: women and children first. My meagre stock of messages soon ran out. Some of them had gone down like a lead balloon, especially in compulsory parade services in England before I was posted overseas.

So here I was in Aden, virtually starting a church from scratch, from the Permanent Staff and temporary National Servicemen of Her Majesty's youngest armed service. How could I get these men interested in the Christian faith and then committed to it?

Something (I would now say: Someone) prompted me to announce that I would give a series of talks over a few months, which would take us right through the Bible ('from Generation to Revolution'!). It was to prove a voyage of discovery for all of us. The Bible became a new book when seen as a whole. To use a well-worn cliché, we had failed to see the wood for the trees. Now God's plan and purpose were unfolding in a fresh way. The men were getting something big enough to sink their teeth into. The thought of being part of a cosmic rescue was a powerful motivation. The Bible story was seen as both real and relevant.

Of course, my 'overview' was at that time quite simple, even naive. I felt like that American tourist who 'did' the British Museum in 20 minutes – and could have done it in 10 if he'd had his running shoes! We raced through the centuries, giving some books of the Bible little more than a passing glance.

But the results surpassed my expectations and set the course for the rest of my life and ministry. I had become a 'Bible teacher', albeit in embryo. My ambition to share the excitement of knowing the whole Bible became a passion.

When I returned to 'normal' church life, I resolved to take my congregation through the whole Bible in a decade (if they put up with me that long). This involved tackling about one 'chapter' at every service. This took a lot of time, both in preparation (an hour in the study for every 10 minutes in the pulpit) and delivery (45–50 minutes). The ratio was similar to that of cooking and eating a meal.

The effect of this systematic 'exposition' of Scripture confirmed its rightness. A real hunger for God's Word was revealed. People began to *come* from far and wide, 'to recharge their batteries' as some explained. Soon this traffic was reversed. Tape recordings, first prepared for the sick and housebound, now began to *go* far and wide, ultimately in hundreds of thousands to 120 countries. No one was more surprised than I.

Leaving Gold Hill in Buckinghamshire for Guildford in Surrey, I found myself sharing in the design and building of the Millmead Centre, which contained an ideal auditorium for continuing this teaching ministry. When it was opened, we decided to associate it with the whole Bible by reading it aloud right through without stopping. It took us 84 hours, from Sunday evening until Thursday morning, each person reading for 15 minutes before passing the Bible on to someone else. We used the 'Living' version, the easiest both to read and to listen to, with the heart as well as the mind.

We did not know what to expect, but the event seemed to capture the public imagination. Even the mayor wanted to take part and by sheer coincidence (or providence) found himself reading about a husband who was 'well known, for he sits in the council chamber with the other civic leaders' (Proverbs 31:23). He insisted on taking a copy home for his wife. Another lady dropped in on her way to see her solicitor about the legal termination of her marriage and found herself reading, 'I hate divorce, says the Lord'. She never went to the lawyer.

An aggregate of 2,000 people attended and bought half a ton of Bibles. Some came for half an hour and were still there hours later, muttering to themselves, 'Well, maybe just one more book and then I really must go.'

It was the first time many, including our most regular attenders, had ever heard a book of the Bible read straight through. In most churches only a few sentences are read each week and then not always consecutively. What other book would get anyone interested, much less excited, if treated in this way?

So on Sundays we worked through the whole Bible book by book. For the Bible is not one book, but many – in fact, it is a whole library (the word *biblia* in Latin and Greek is plural: 'books'). And not just many books, but many *kinds* of books – history, law, letters, songs, etc. It became necessary, when we had finished studying one book, and were starting on another, to begin with a special introduction covering very basic questions: What kind of book is this? When was it written? Who wrote it? Who was it written for? Above all, *why* was it written? The answer to that last question provided the 'key' to unlock its message. Nothing in that book could be fully understood unless seen as part of the whole. The context of every 'text' was not just the paragraph or the section but fundamentally the whole book itself.

By now, I was becoming more widely known as a Bible teacher and was invited to colleges, conferences and conventions – at first in this country, but increasingly overseas, where tapes had opened doors and prepared the way. I enjoy meeting new people and seeing new places, but the novelty of sitting in a jumbo jet wears off in 10 minutes!

Everywhere I went I found the same eager desire to know God's Word. I praised God for the invention of recording cassettes which, unlike video systems, are standardized the world over. They were helping to plug a real hole in so many places. There is so much successful evangelism but so little teaching ministry to stabilize, develop and mature converts.

I might have continued along these lines until the end of my active ministry, but the Lord had another surprise for me, which was the last link in the chain that led to the publication of these volumes.

In the early 1990s, Bernard Thompson, a friend pastoring a church in Wallingford, near Oxford, asked me to speak at a short series of united meetings with the aim of increasing interest in and knowledge of the Bible – an objective guaranteed to hook me!

I said I would come once a month and speak for three hours about one book in the Bible (with a coffee break in the middle!). In return, I asked those attending to read that book right through before and after my visit. During the following weeks preachers were to base their sermons and house group discussions on the same book. All this would hopefully mean familiarity at least with that one book.

My purpose was two-fold. On the one hand, to get people so interested in that book that they could hardly wait to read it. On the other hand, to give them enough insight and information so that when they did read it they would be excited by their ability to understand it. To help with both, I used pictures, charts, maps and models.

This approach really caught on. After just four months I was pressed to book dates for the next five years, to cover all 66 books! I laughingly declined, saying I might be in heaven long before then (in fact, I have rarely booked anything more than six months ahead, not wanting to mortgage the future, or presume that I have one). But the Lord had other plans and enabled me to complete the marathon.

Anchor Recordings (72, The Street, Kennington, Ashford, Kent TN24 9HS) have distributed my tapes for the last 20 years and when the Director, Jim Harris, heard the recordings of these meetings, he urged me to consider putting them on video. He arranged for cameras and crew to come to High Leigh Conference Centre, its main hall 'converted' into a studio, for three days at a time, enabling 18 programmes to be made with an invited audience. It took another five years to complete this project, which was distributed under the title 'Unlocking the Bible'.

Now these videos are travelling around the world. They are being used in house groups, churches, colleges, the armed forces, gypsy camps, prisons and on cable television networks. During an extended visit to Malaysia, they were being snapped up at a rate of a thousand a week. They have infiltrated all six continents, including Antartica!

More than one have called this my 'legacy to the church'. Certainly it is the fruit of many years' work. And I am now in my seventieth year on planet earth, though I do not think the Lord has finished with me yet. But I did think this particular task had reached its conclusion. I was mistaken.

HarperCollins approached me with a view to publishing this material in a series of volumes. For the last decade or so I had been writing books for other publishers, so was already convinced that this was a good means of spreading God's Word. Nevertheless, I had two huge reservations about this proposal which made me very hesitant. One was due to the way the material had been prepared and the other related to the way it had been delivered. I shall explain them in reverse order.

First, I have never written out in full any sermon, lecture or talk. I speak from notes, sometimes pages of them. I have been concerned about communication as much as content and intuitively knew that a full manuscript interrupts the rapport between speaker and audience, not least by diverting his eyes from the listeners. Speech that is more spontaneous can respond to reactions as well as express more emotions.

The result is that my speaking and writing styles are very different, each adapted to its own function. I enjoy listening to my tapes and can be deeply moved by myself. I am enthusiastic about reading one of my new publications, often telling my wife, 'This really *is* good stuff!' But when I read a transcript of what I have said, I am ashamed and even appalled. Such repetition of words and phrases! Such rambling, even incomplete sentences! Such a mixture of verb tenses, particularly past and present! Do I really abuse the Queen's English like this? The evidence is irrefutable.

I made it clear that I could not possibly contemplate writing out all this material in full. It has taken most of one lifetime anyway and I do not have another. True, transcripts of the talks had already been made, with a view to translating and dubbing the videos into other languages such as Spanish and Chinese. But the thought of these being printed as they were horrified me. Perhaps this is a final struggle with pride, but the contrast with my written books, over which I took such time and trouble, was more than I could bear.

I was assured that copy editors correct most grammatical blunders. But the main remedy proposed was to employ a 'ghostwriter' who was in tune with me and my ministry, to adapt the material for printing. An introduction to the person chosen, Andy Peck, gave me every confidence that he could do the job, even though the result would not be what I would have written – nor, for that matter, what he would have written himself.

I gave him all the notes, tapes, videos and transcripts, but these volumes are as much his work as mine. He has worked incredibly hard and I am deeply grateful to him for enabling me to reach many more with the truth that sets people free. If one gets a prophet's reward for merely giving the prophet a drink of water, I can only thank the Lord for the reward Andy will get for this immense labour of love.

Second, I have never kept careful records of my sources. This is partly because the Lord blessed me with a reasonably good memory for such things as quotations and illustrations and perhaps also because I have never used secretarial assistance.

Books have played a major role in my work – three tons of them, according to the last furniture remover we employed, filling two rooms and a garden shed. They are in three categories: those I have read, those I intend to read and those I will never read! They have been such a blessing to me and such a bane to my wife.

The largest section by far is filled with Bible commentaries. When preparing a Bible study, I have looked up all relevant writers, but only after I have prepared as much as I can on my own. Then I have both added to and corrected my efforts in the light of scholarly and devotional writings.

It would be impossible to name all those to whom I have been indebted. Like many others I devoured William Barclay's *Daily Bible Readings* as soon as they were issued back in the 1950s. His knowledge of New Testament background and vocabulary was invaluable and his simple and clear style a model to follow, though I later came to question his 'liberal' interpretations. John Stott, Merill Tenney, Gordon Fee and William Hendrickson were among those who opened up the New Testament for me, while Alec Motyer, G. T. Wenham and Derek Kidner did the same for the Old. And time would fail to tell of Denney, Lightfoot, Nygren, Robinson, Adam Smith, Howard, Ellison, Mullen, Ladd, Atkinson, Green, Beasley-Murray, Snaith, Marshall, Morris, Pink and many many others. Nor must I forget two remarkable little books from the pens of women: *What the Bible is all about* by Henrietta Mears and *Christ in all the Scriptures* by A. M. Hodgkin. To have sat at their feet has been an inestimable privilege. I have always regarded a willingness to learn as one of the fundamental qualifications to be a teacher.

I soaked up all these sources like a sponge. I remembered so much of *what* I read, but could not easily recall *where* I had read it. This did not seem to matter too much when gathering material for preaching, since most of these writers were precisely aiming to help preachers and did not expect to be constantly quoted. Indeed, a sermon full of attributed quotations can be distracting, if not misinterpreted as name-dropping or indirectly claiming to be well read. As could my previous paragraph!

But printing, unlike preaching, is subject to copyright, since royalties are involved. And the fear of breaching this held me back from allowing any of my spoken ministry to be reproduced in print. It would be out of the question to trace back 40 years' scrounging and even if that were possible, the necessary footnotes and acknowledgements could double the size and price of these volumes.

The alternative was to deny access to my material for those who could most benefit from it, which my publisher persuaded me would be wrong. At least I was responsible for collecting and collating it all, but I dare to believe that there is sufficient original contribution to justify its release.

I can only offer an apology and my gratitude to all those whose studies I have plundered over the years, whether in small or large amounts, hoping they might see this as an example of that imitation which is the sincerest form of flattery. To use another quotation I read somewhere: 'Certain authors, speaking of their works, say "my book" … They would do better to say "our book" … because there is in them usually more of other people's than their own' (the original came from Pascal).

So here is 'our' book! I suppose I am what the French bluntly call a 'vulgarizer'. That is someone who takes what the academics teach and makes it simple enough for the 'common' people to understand. I am content with that. As one old lady said to me, after I had expounded a quite profound passage of Scripture, 'You broke it up small enough for us to take it in.' I have, in fact, always aimed so to teach that a 12-year-old boy could understand and remember my message.

Some readers will be disappointed, even frustrated, with the paucity of text references, especially if they want to check me out! But their absence is intentional. God gave us his Word in books, but not in chapters and verses. That was the work of two bishops, French and Irish, centuries later. It became easier to find a 'text' and to ignore context. How many Christians who quote John 3:16 can recite verses 15 and 17? Many no longer 'search the scriptures'; they simply look them up (given the numbers). So I have followed the apostles' habit of naming the authors only – 'as Isaiah or David or Samuel said'. For example, the Bible says that God whistles. Where on earth does it say that? In the book of Isaiah. Whereabouts? Go and find out for yourself. Then you'll also find out when he did and why he did. And you'll have the satisfaction of having discovered all that by yourself.

One final word. Behind my hope that these introductions to the Bible books will help you to get to know and love them more than you did lies a much greater and deeper longing – that you will also come to know better and love more the subject of all the books, the Lord Himself. I was deeply touched by the remark of someone who had watched all the videos within a matter of days: 'I know so much more about the Bible now, but the biggest thing was that I felt the heart of God as never before.'

What more could a Bible teacher ask? May you experience the same as you read these pages and join me in saying: Praise Father, Son and Holy Spirit.

J. David Pawson
Sherborne St John, 2000

Yes, I thought I knew my Bible,
Reading piecemeal, hit or miss:
Now a part of John or Matthew,
Then a bit of Genesis.

Certain chapters of Isaiah,
Certain psalms, the twenty-third,
First of Proverbs, twelfth of Romans –
Yes, I thought I knew the Word.

But I found that thorough reading
Was a different thing to do
And the way was unfamiliar
When I read my Bible through.

You who like to play at Bible,
Dip and dabble here and there,
Just before you kneel all weary,
Yawning through a hurried prayer.

You who treat this crown of writings
As you treat no other book:
Just a paragraph disjointed,
Just a crude impatient look.

Try a worthier procedure,
Try a broad and steady view;
You will kneel in awesome wonder
When you read the Bible through.

Author unknown

PART I

HEBREWS

Introduction

Difficult or delightful?

Among modern readers opinion about the Letter to the Hebrews is very divided. Some find it one of the most difficult letters of the New Testament. This is partly because, to Gentile eyes, it is a very Jewish letter, describing sacrifices, altars and priestly matters in some detail. A proper understanding of Hebrews requires a familiarity with the Old Testament Scriptures, especially the Book of Leviticus, which most Gentiles don't have. In addition, some of the arguments in Hebrews don't touch the modern mind. Who cares about angels and genealogies? They are hardly a major topic of conversation, even among Christians.

Furthermore, the Greek of the Letter to the Hebrews is very complicated, though it is widely regarded as the best Greek in the New Testament. The New Testament was written not in classical Greek but in *koine* Greek, the language of the streets as opposed to the language of the university. But Hebrews is nearer to the classical language than any other part of the New Testament. Even in English translation the language is refined and sophisticated, and for some this represents a barrier.

But Hebrews has its supporters. Some say it is the most delightful book in the whole Bible. They love it and revel in it, usually for one of three reasons.

1. THE MAGNIFICENT CHAPTER ON FAITH

This chapter is like taking a walk through a mausoleum, as the reader looks back into the past to the lives of the great heroes of faith. To those who find the detailed argument of the earlier chapters a bit tough, chapter 11 is something of a relief. At last there is something that registers with them.

2. THE LIGHT SHED ON THE OLD TESTAMENT

Hebrews deals with the question of how the Old Testament and the New Testament relate. It explains how we should treat the Law of Moses, as it unfolds the relationship of our Christian faith to the ritual of the temple and shows how the people of God have entered a new era of relationship with God. As such it provides many interpretive models for our understanding of the Old Testament as Christians.

3. WHAT IT TELLS US ABOUT CHRIST

Those who love Jesus love Hebrews, because it throws a light on him that no other part of the New Testament does. A favourite word of the writer of Hebrews is 'better'. Jesus is described as 'better' rather than 'the best' (though that is also true), because he is being compared with lesser alternatives that were attractive to the original readership. Jesus is better than the angels, better than the prophets, better than all other intermediaries.

The opinions that this is a difficult or a delightful book are really both extreme positions that miss the main point of the letter. The real key to Hebrews is the question, 'Why was it written?' Though it is a little complicated to find the answer, once you have found it, the whole letter opens up.

Who was the author?

But before we look at why the letter was written, we need to consider who wrote it. One scholar called this 'the riddle of the New Testament', for it is the only New Testament book whose authorship is definitely unknown. There have been all sorts of guesses. Some older versions of the King James translation of the Bible call it 'the Epistle of Paul to the Hebrews', but this is sheer guesswork. I don't think Paul wrote it. It is not his style or his language. Others have suggested that it might have been written by Barnabas, in part because of the large amount of encouragement within its pages. Some say Stephen, others support Silas or Apollos. One suggestion is that the author was Priscilla, and the lack of a name was to conceal the fact that a woman wrote it, though I think this is very unlikely. Ultimately I have to say – with the great church Father, Origen of Alexandria – God alone knows who wrote it!

Where was the letter sent to?

We are also uncertain where the letter was sent. The only address on it is 'to the Hebrews', which is hardly specific! Once again there are many suggestions. Some say it was sent to Alexandria, others say Antioch or Jerusalem or Ephesus. We cannot be certain, but there is a big clue right at the end. The writer says that 'everyone *from* Italy sends greetings'. So I think it is a sensible deduction to say it was sent *to* Italy, which suggests that it was meant for the church in Rome.

Yet we can clearly see that the Letter to the Hebrews was written a bit later than the Letter to the Romans, because Hebrews refers to certain things that had not yet happened when Paul wrote Romans. So I am assuming that Hebrews was written to the Christians in Rome and, in view of the title, to that half of the church that was Jewish. But this raises the question, 'Why would a letter be needed for half the church?'

When was the letter sent?

Clearly, the first leaders of the church in Rome have died, because near the end of the letter the writer says, 'remember your leaders'. The temple and its sacrifices were still in operation, because the writer talks about them in the present tense. So he must have written the letter before AD 70, when the temple was destroyed and the sacrifices ceased. So Hebrews was written after Paul wrote to the Romans in AD 55 and before AD 70.

Nero

The reason for the writing of the letter becomes clear when we consider what happened during this period. The situation had changed considerably since the time of Paul's Letter to the Romans, largely because of Nero's accession to the imperial throne. We noted in our study of Romans (see *Unlocking the Bible: New Testament Book 2*, HarperCollins, 2000) that under Claudius some 10,000 Jews were banished from Rome in the early AD 50s, before Paul wrote his letter. (It was at this point that Priscilla and Aquila fled to Corinth, as mentioned in Acts.) The church in Rome became increasingly Gentile as a result, so that when the Jews returned after the death of Claudius in AD 54, tensions were developing between the Jewish believers and those with a Gentile background, who were now leading the fellowship. We saw in our study of Romans that Paul wrote to help the Jews to reintegrate alongside their Gentile brethren.

But Nero's reign was a time of great suffering for the church. Nero, like Hitler, did some good things in the beginning. If you read the life of Hitler, you will find that he saved Germany from unemployment and inflation, built great roads, and ordered the production of the Volkswagen Beetle as 'the people's car'. In the same way, when you read the history of Nero, you find that he did a lot of good things for Rome in the beginning. He listened to other people's advice and was able to rule wisely. But there came a point when Nero stopped listening and became a dictator. Just as Hitler wanted to rebuild Berlin, so Nero wanted to rebuild Rome. He had big ideas for pulling everything down and building the grandest buildings that had ever been built. In short, he became a megalomaniac, and the people who began to suffer more than anybody else were the Christians, and many of them were killed by Nero.

In the Letter to the Romans there is no trace of persecution. The church has to fight immorality in Rome, but there isn't yet any direct persecution. But in the Letter to the Hebrews there is one section which tells us the kind of persecution they were already suffering. None of them had yet been martyred, which means we are in the middle of Nero's reign. Their homes were being vandalized. Their possessions were being confiscated. Some of them had been in prison – hence the reference towards the end of the letter to visiting 'those who are in prison'. Timothy is mentioned as one of those who had been imprisoned and released. So it was getting pretty tough to be a Christian. It wasn't costing them their lives at this point, but it was costing them pretty well everything else.

Jewish believers

Of course, this was happening to all the believers, whether they were Gentiles or Jews, so why was this letter written only to the Jewish believers? The answer is very simple and explains the whole letter. The Jews had a way of escape from suffering that was not open to the Gentile believers. The Jewish believers could get out of trouble by going back to the synagogue. At this time Christianity was illegal, but Judaism was still legal, with synagogues officially 'registered'. The church was an underground church, rather as in the Communist era in Russia and China, and in some parts of the Muslim world today.

So the Jewish believers could return to the synagogue and so take their families out of persecution. They could even claim to be going back to the same God. But the cost of doing it – indeed, the only way for them to get back into the Jewish synagogue – was to publicly deny their faith in Jesus. It was a great dilemma. They had heard about Jesus and believed he was the Messiah. But having joined the church, they now found their children being persecuted at school, their windows being smashed and their property being confiscated. They knew that if they took their families back into the synagogue they would be safe. But they would have to say in front of the synagogue, 'I deny that Jesus is the Messiah.'

So the letter is written primarily to Jewish believers against the background of persecution. The writer uses sailing metaphors to urge them to stand firm – 'don't pull up your anchors, don't drift away, don't lower your sails' – which may suggest that he had a sailing background.

Exhortation and exposition

At the end he says he has written a 'short letter of exhortation'. It is certainly a letter of exhortation, but it is not very short! An exhortation is very practical. He is not trying to teach them doctrine, but is trying to stop this drift back to the synagogue. Everything he says from beginning to end is aimed at that problem. He throws everything at them. He appeals to them, warns them, speaks tenderly yet strongly. He uses every argument he can, because he fears they will lose their salvation if they go back to Judaism.

Appreciating this passionate appeal will save us from seeing the book as a doctrinal exposition. Many preachers I have heard expound this letter as if it were purely a study of Christ, and they miss the practical element. According to the *Oxford English Dictionary*, the word 'exhort' means 'to admonish urgently, to urge someone to a course of action'. The whole letter is urging people to a particular course of action. The appeal is both negative and positive: 'Please don't go back, but do go on.'

There's a true story of someone who died in the potholes of Yorkshire. This is what the coroner said at the inquest: 'If he had just kept moving he would be alive today.' Instead he sat down and stayed in one place, and hypothermia set in. This is the message of the Letter to the Hebrews: 'Keep moving!'

But this is not the language of rebuke. The author identifies with his readers. He says, 'Let us go on', putting himself alongside them. Indeed, he calls himself a paraclete (which is also the title given to the Holy Spirit in John's Gospel and means 'standby, strengthener'). We might think of him as a climber going back for someone at the end of the rope and climbing with them to help them reach the summit.

The pattern of the letter is unusual for the New Testament, as the writer constantly alternates between exposition and exhortation. (Most of the New Testament books have doctrine first and application second.) He is constantly arguing and appealing, and the proportions of the argument and the appeal change as we go through the letter.

In chapters 1 and 2 we have a long argument and a short appeal. But gradually, as you read the book there are shorter arguments and longer appeals, until chapter 11 gives a short exposition, followed by a long appeal in chapters 12 and 13. So the writer presents more argument and less appeal at the beginning, and less argument and more appeal at the end. This is one reason why the earlier part is a little more difficult to understand than the later.

The appeal sections are replete with the phrase 'Let us …' For example: 'Let us lay aside every handicap and keep running, looking to Jesus'; 'Let us go on'; 'Let us go for the finish'; 'Let us go for the prize'. 'Let us' occurs thirteen times in the whole letter, but eight times in this last section. It is a great build-up to a personal appeal, which would move all but the most hard-hearted.

Most of the arguments are taken from the Old Testament, which was the only Scripture they then had (apart from Paul's Letter to the Romans). So these arguments would have been readily accepted by the Jewish believers. The writer treats the Old Testament in two ways: negatively, contrasting the inferior life under the Old Covenant with that enjoyed by the New Covenant believer; and positively, noting the continuity between the Testaments and the many examples we can emulate. To quote Augustine, 'The New is in the Old concealed, the Old is in the New revealed.'

Language and structure

Many find the language and structure of Hebrews difficult to grasp. The diagram opposite will help us. It gives us an outline of the shape of chapters 1–2, showing the division between heaven and earth. God in heaven spoke his words through angels and to the prophets in bits and pieces. You can piece together the whole of the life of Jesus from the Old Testament. It is like a jigsaw puzzle when the box is first opened. The prophets gave the word to men, but in fact that word brought death to them, for the word of the Law brought death.

Next we see how 'in these last days he has spoken to us through his Son who died.' The Son has spoken to us through the apostles. We hear the words of the prophets in the Old Testament and the words of the apostles in the New Testament.

Jesus became a man, died and then returned to heaven as our Pioneer. 'Pioneer' is a favourite title for Jesus in the Letter to the Hebrews. It means 'the Trailblazer', the one who went

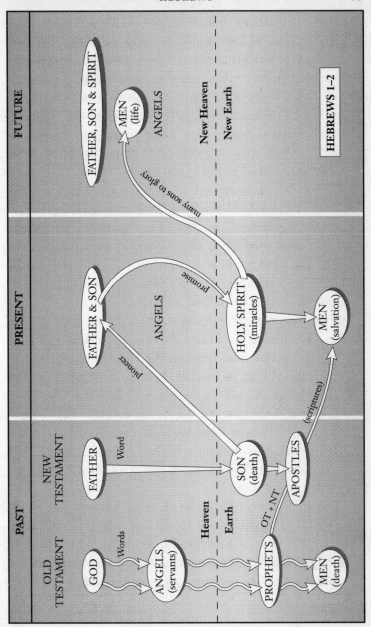

ahead in order for us to follow. He did all this so that we might follow him back to heaven. We are also told that he is now above the angels. A man had never been above the angels until Jesus ascended. From this exalted position he has poured out the promised Holy Spirit upon us, enabling miracles to be done. Men may therefore follow the Pioneer and finish up above the angels, taking their place among the many sons whom Jesus will bring to glory. So believers are going to be above the angels, and served by the angels.

The shape of chapters 4–10 is rather more complicated. We must remember that Hebrew thinking is horizontal time-line thinking, between the past, the present and the future, whereas Greek thinking is more space-oriented thinking – a vertical line between heaven and earth. The Letter to the Hebrews combines these two outlooks, and this is why the outline opposite may seem difficult to grasp.

So we have the vertical line between the heavenly and the earthly, the invisible world and the visible world, and we have the horizontal time-line between the Old Covenant and the New Covenant. They all meet at the cross. Faith takes us from the earthly and the old to the heavenly and the new. Faith brings us out of the past and the earthly into the heavenly and the future. The bottom-right quadrant reminds us that you can fall back in the other direction. You can go back from the New Covenant into the Old; you can return from the heavenly into the earthly again.

The old sacrifices had to be repeated; the new sacrifice is once for all. The old priests are on one side; the one Priest, Jesus, of the order of Melchizedek, is on the other. The old sanctuary has its closed tabernacle, and the new sanctuary has its open throne – we can come right into the Holy of Holies now.

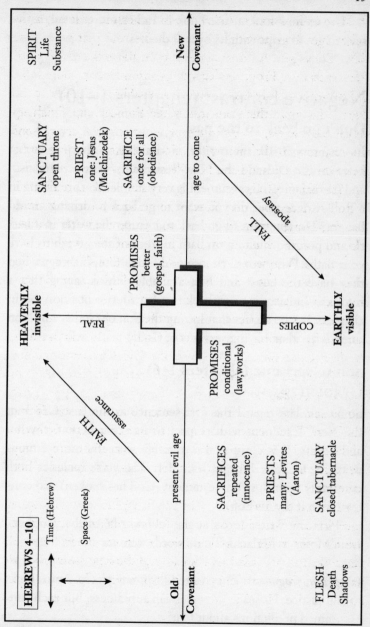

Let us now look at the book in rather more detail, as we seek to get to grips with its overall themes.

Negative contrast (chapters 1–10)

Don't go back to the past

In chapters 1–10 the writer is drawing a sharp contrast between the Old and the New Testaments, between Judaism and Christianity. His argument is very simple. You are riding in a Rolls-Royce now; do you want to go back to driving an old banger? Do you want to go back to heating the water in a kettle and pouring it into a tin bath in front of the hearth to have your bath? Who would choose to do such foolish things when they have the latest and best available? He is saying that a return to Judaism is to go back to a far inferior position. So in chapters 1–6 he argues that having the Son of God is a million times *better* than having servants of God.

Son to servants (chapters 1–6)

1. PROPHETS (1:1–3)

Some scholars regard the first sentence as the best Greek in the New Testament with respect to its construction, rhythm and beauty. It is compared favourably with the more famous words in Genesis 1:1 and John 1:1. The verse includes both continuity with the Old Testament (God has spoken) and contrast with it (by his Son).

First the writer looks at the 'old words' of the prophets, from Moses to Malachi. These words were in:

(a) *Many fragments*. They were like jigsaw pieces. Amos looks at justice, Hosea at mercy, Isaiah at holiness. But each contained predictions about Christ.

(b) *Many forms*. The picture on the lid of the 'jigsaw' varied too. There was prose, poetry, prediction, history, parable, law, love-songs and visions. The communication was through ordinary men and women from a wide range of social backgrounds.

Then the writer compares these previous methods with the 'new words'. He says that in these 'last days' (i.e. in the final period of history, since the coming of Christ) God has given us a final means of communication. This 'Word' has been given to us as believers. This time it was not fragmentary but 'by a Son'. He goes on to give us a three-dimensional view of Jesus.

(a) Creation

(i) *He gets it all in the end.* God has made Jesus the heir of all things. So the Son will one day have it all. Psalm 2:8 speaks of the nations being his inheritance. So the One whose own clothes were gambled for at the end of his first visit will return and reign over all kingdoms and peoples.

(ii) *He made it all in the beginning.* This Son started it all. He was not just a humble carpenter, but was there at the very beginning as the Creator, initiating and deciding upon creation.

(iii) *He keeps it all going meanwhile*. While he was on earth he demonstrated his power to 'still the storm'. In his risen life, he is at the helm of the universe, holding it all together.

(b) Creator

(i) We see a *reflection of his brightness*. Just as sunshine is to the sun, so his glory is to the Son. Glory is part of his intrinsic being.

(ii) He is the *stamp of God's likeness*. Just as a seal is made by an impression, so Christ is the exact impression of God. When we see Jesus, we see the Father.

(c) Creature

(i) *Saviour on a cross*. Despite all we have said, this glorious Son died on a cross. In so doing he made purification for sins. This time it was not by a word, but by his action, allowing himself to be a sacrifice. This was his work. Not even his Father, God, could share it with him.

(ii) *Lord with a crown*. But he did not remain dead. He was raised and glorified. He is the Lord, ascended above all and at the helm of the universe – the Prince of Peace, the Prophet, Priest and King at the right hand of God. This exalted position of Jesus leads the writer naturally on to the next section, where he looks at the Son with respect to angelic beings.

2. ANGELS (1:4–2:8)

Scripture depicts angels as heavenly, spiritual and supernatural beings above man and below God. They are the highest created order. Although they were revered within Judaism, the writer argues that they are just ministering servants. He is asking his readers, 'Do you want to go back to the stage where the only contact you have got with heaven is through angels? You have got the Son – you can't get closer to the Father than that.'

The Jews gave the angels an exalted status as intermediaries or messengers. Christians, however, tend to think too little of angels. Therefore it was necessary for the writer to compare Christ with the angels, so that the readers would see both in their true light.

(a) Present – he didn't sit with angels (1:4–14)
Christ had a superior position to angelic beings. The writer demonstrates this with a series of questions and quotations from the Old Testament.

(b) Past – he didn't speak by angels (2:1–4)

The old angelic words were binding, for they came with divine authority. This new communication is even more serious.

(i) Direct communication. It comes at the horizontal level. The word is given by the apostles, who are eye-witnesses to Christ. They saw and heard the message that they proclaim.

(ii) Divine confirmation. At the same time, this was not merely 'human' communication, but signs, wonders and miracles confirmed the word. So there is an urgency about receiving and responding to the word. It provides the moorings we need if we are not to drift away.

(c) Future – he didn't suffer for angels (2:5–18)

(i) The world subject to man (2:5–9). Man was placed on earth to rule the universe. In Genesis 1:28 we read that he was given dominion over all the creatures of the earth, the air and the sea. Psalm 8:4–6 reinforces this position. But in reality we do not see mankind in general ruling over all – except that Jesus became a man and fulfils in himself the design of God for mankind.

(ii) Man subject to death (2:10–18). We are reminded that man is subject to death and that this fear of death is used by Satan to keep us in bondage. Jesus knows what it is like to be human, having lived on earth as a 'flesh and blood' man, and continuing to be a human, though now in his exalted state. As such he can sympathize with men and women who face struggles similar to those that he faced.

3. APOSTLES (3:1–4:13)

An apostle is someone 'sent' by God to fulfil a task, as were Moses and Joshua. But Jesus was a 'better' apostle than both of them, 'sent' for a greater purpose.

(a) Moses – out of Egypt (3:1–18)

Moses is generally regarded by Jews as one of their greatest leaders, but Jesus is even greater. At the Transfiguration in the Gospels, Jesus meets with Moses and Elijah, but he is clearly the superior one.

(i)   Faithful house. In Hebrew the word 'house' means both 'building' and 'family', rather as 'the House of Windsor' means the generations that belong to the royal family. Jesus is described as 'builder of a faithful house'. We are the stones who are part of the building. But the writer asks whether we are as faithful in our faith as Moses and Jesus were.

(ii) Faithless hearts. Sadly, Israel failed in their task of being faithful to God. Only two people out of 2.5 million got into the Promised Land. The leaders were good but the followers were not.

The problem was unbelief, which led to disobedience and finally to apostasy and destruction. They failed to 'enter the rest'. The history of Israel represents a warning to New Testament believers. The people rebelled at Massah (Exodus 17:1–7) and gave in to testing at Meribah (Numbers 20:1–13). In both cases the problem was lack of water.

The writer warns that the readers can do the same thing themselves. They can become hardened by sin. The same fate will befall them that befell the people in the Old Testament, for God will be angry with all who are disobedient (cf. Romans 11:22).

(b) Joshua – into Canaan (4:1–13)

The 'land of rest' was to be a land of rest from disease, slavery, invasion and poverty. They would also have a day of rest and celebration every week – the Sabbath. They were also supposed to know rest from spiritual struggle (Deuteronomy 12:9; Joshua 1:13). But that last rest was never entered into, so remains to be claimed.

(i) The work of God (4:1–10). On the seventh day of creation, God was no longer at work in creation. The description of this day is different to the other six in that it omits evening and morning, leaving some to speculate that there may be a special significance attached to it, beyond the fact that it is a day of rest. The Sabbath day, when God ceases from his work, portrays a God who is always at peace and rest in himself.

(ii) The word of God (4:11–13). Faith can be defined as the right response to the word of God. The word is living, like the God who speaks it; it is active, in that its blessings and curses affect people; it is sharp, like a Roman two edged sword; it is piercing, able to divide joints and marrow; it is discerning, able to get to the truth of a matter.

Jesus is like Moses in that he brings his people out, but also like Joshua in that he leads his people into the Promised Land. This is a reminder that it is important not only to remember what we have been saved from, but also to consider what we have been saved for.

Substance to shadows (chapters 7–10)

Having argued that the Son is better than the servants, the writer then changes his approach, and in chapters 7–10 we have the remarkable argument that the substance is better than the shadows.

This is perhaps best illustrated by the story of *Daddy Long Legs*, originally a book by Jean Webster and now a film. It is the story of a little girl in an orphanage. She knows that there is a wealthy man who provides for the orphanage. One day she sees his shadow on a wall, and, because it is an elongated shadow with tremendously long legs, due to the position of the light, she calls the shadow 'Daddy Long Legs'. For years she dreams of this shadow. But one day she meets him and falls in love with him. He too falls for her and their relationship develops.

The point is this. Once she has got him, she stops thinking about the shadow altogether, because the substance is better than the shadow. What would you think of her if she went back to the shadow on the wall and tried to kiss it, now that she knows the real man?

In the Old Testament there are many 'shadows' of Jesus. Some people call them 'types', but I prefer to call them shadows. It is as if Jesus cast his shadow back into the Old Testament, but since a shadow is always distorted, it never quite gives you the clear picture that you want.

When we read the Old Testament there is a sense in which we are reading about the shadows of Jesus. Here are three examples of what I mean.

1. PRIESTHOOD (MELCHIZEDEK)

In the Book of Leviticus we are looking at many shadows of Jesus. The sacrifices are the shadow of the sacrifice he made for sin at the cross. The animal sacrifices are shadows of Jesus, who is described in the New Testament as the Passover Lamb. The priesthood of Aaron and his family is a shadow of Christ's priestly work of intercession for us.

Jesus is also clearly shadowed in the Book of Genesis by Melchizedek – the mysterious priest-king who reigned over Jerusalem centuries before it was taken by the Jews, and who gave bread and wine to Abraham.

2. COVENANT (NEW)

But there is also the shadow of God's covenantal relationship with his people through Christ. The writer asks why they were considering going back to the Old Covenant now that they were in the New. The New Covenant was, after all, based on forgiveness and what I call 'forgetness'. I think the most amazing miracle is that when God forgives, he also forgets.

When I was a Pastor at the Millmead Centre in Guildford, there was a Sunday when everyone had gone home after the service, but there was a little old lady sitting in the church all by herself, crying her heart out. I went and sat by her and asked what her problem was. She explained that years ago she did a dreadful thing, and that if her family and friends knew about it they would never speak to her again. She said that for 30 years she had been asking God to forgive her, and he never had. I told her that the very first time she asked him, he forgave it and he forgot it. So for 30 years he hadn't known what she was talking about! She told me she didn't believe it. I took her through some scriptures which spoke of the New Covenant and how God would no longer remember her sins. It took 20 minutes to convince her that God had forgotten all about it. She got up, and I couldn't believe my eyes – she danced around the church! She was about 70, and here she was, dancing around the church for sheer joy. God had forgotten it! Our trouble is, we can't forget it, and so we struggle to forgive ourselves.

3. SACRIFICE (CROSS)

We also see a shadow when Abraham offered Isaac as a sacrifice. Many assume that this incident took place when Isaac was a young boy, but he was actually in his early thirties. Every Jewish picture of the scene shows a full-grown man who could easily have overcome his father, but instead submitted to him.

Our failure to realize his age is caused partly by chapter divisions. We miss the next incident in the next chapter, which talks of Sarah's death and tells us how old Isaac was when she died. So Isaac was around 33, and the mountain – Mount Moriah – was the very mountain on which Jesus died on the cross. The parallels are very clear. In the event, of course, an angel stopped Abraham, and a ram with its head caught in thorns was sacrificed on that mountain. Centuries later, the Lamb of God had his head crowned with thorns and was offered on Mount Moriah.

So the writer impresses upon them the inferiority of a return to Judaism, with its repetitive sacrifices and its inferior covenant. If they returned to Judaism, they would be rejecting the once-for-all sacrifice of Jesus.

Positive continuity (chapters 11–13)

Go on into the future

We now turn to the positive side in the second half of the letter, where the author draws a contrast between the Old and New Testaments. He emphasizes the continuity between the Old and the New. There are good things in the Old that are not obsolete – some things follow straight through.

Faith in God

One common theme is the theme of faith. When we consider the resources that the Old Testament heroes had, their faith leaves us standing. They didn't have any of the revelation we have in Christ. They didn't have the pouring out of the Holy Spirit. And yet those men went on believing, even though they never saw what they believed in. So we have a kind of double relationship to the Old Testament. There are some things we leave behind, because they are shadows and we now have the substance. But there are some things we need to emulate, particularly in this area of faith. The writer goes through group after group in the Old Testament:

- Abel, Enoch and Noah.
- Abraham, Isaac and Jacob. (God has tied his name to those three human names. He will always be known as the God of Abraham, Isaac and Jacob.)
- Joseph and Moses.
- Joshua and Rahab. (Rahab is the first woman in the list. She was a prostitute and a Gentile, but she staked her whole future on God's people, hiding the spies in Jericho. She is held up as an example of faith, not only in the Letter to the Hebrews, but also in the Letter of James. She appears in the genealogy of Jesus, for she was the great-great-grandmother of David.)
- Gideon, Barak, Samson and Jephthah.
- David.
- Samuel and the prophets.

There are two things we must note about this list of believers:

1 Their faith was shown in what they did. By faith Noah built an ark; by faith Abraham lived in tents for the rest of his life; by faith Moses gave up the ease of Egypt, and so on. As James puts it in his epistle, 'Show me your faith by your works.' Real faith shows itself in action.

2 The second thing that is important to note is that all these men were still living by faith when they died, yet they never saw what they believed in. Faith to them wasn't just a one-off decision at a crusade, but an on-going trust that

continued until they died, even if they never saw what was promised.

At the end of chapter 11 there is a tremendous reminder that these great heroes of the faith are waiting for us to catch up with them. Then we will join them in seeing what they were believing for! So, for example, Abraham left a very comfortable two-storey home, with heating and running water, to obey the voice of God. Archaeologists have dug out the houses of Abraham's home area, Ur of the Chaldees, and they were the most up-to-date, comfortable homes you can imagine. Abraham was 80 when God told him that he must leave his house to live in a tent for the rest of his life. Imagine how you would feel if you had a nice, comfortable, centrally heated bungalow by the sea, and God said he wanted you to leave your relatives and friends and live in a tent in the mountains for the rest of your life! Yet Abraham did it, by faith. And one day we will join him in enjoying all that God has for his people.

Focus on Jesus

But our attention must not be on Abraham, or any of the other great heroes of faith. We must fix our eyes on Jesus! In the closing chapters the writer focuses on three areas in which we should focus on Jesus.

1   Pioneer and perfecter of our faith. Forget about the spectators – there is somebody standing at the finishing-post who actually fired the pistol at the starting-line. He is the one who started us off, and he will be the one who will see us finish. The message is, 'Keep your eyes fixed on Jesus and run!'

2   Mediator of a New Covenant. Valuable though the Old
    Covenant was, it was inferior to the one that God brought
    in through Jesus.
3   Sufferer outside the camp. Jesus needed to be prepared to
    die a criminal's death in order for our salvation to be
    secure, literally an outcast among his own people.

'Problem passages'

Having taken an overview of the book, let us now look at
what are considered to be the 'problem passages' of Hebrews
– though it is worth noting that the label 'problem passage'
is generally given to passages that don't fit in with what the
readers already believe! I am constantly being asked, for
example, 'What do you think about Paul's problem passages
on women?' I don't think there are any problem passages on
women. They are only 'problems' to those who disagree with
them!

   The so-called 'problem' in Hebrews concerns the suggestion that believers may fall away from faith in Jesus and not be
saved on the final day. The best known of these warnings is
found in Hebrews chapter 6. But the letter also includes several
other severe warnings to those who drift away (see 2:1–2;
3:5–6, 12–14; 6:4–8, 11–12; 10:23–30, 35–39; 12:14–17).
These verses represent a thread running all the way through
the letter, which starts in chapter 2 with the words, 'How shall
we escape if we neglect so great a salvation?' Every time I have
heard that quoted, it has been quoted against sinners who are
neglecting the gospel. But the 'we' here refers to Christian
believers. The writer is saying that all we need to do to get into
danger is to neglect our salvation. Most churches have members who have drifted away.

This theme continues with two passages in chapter 3, the long one in chapter 6, and another in chapter 10, which says, 'If we deliberately keep on sinning after we have received the knowledge of the truth, no sacrifice for sins is left ...' This has led some commentators to conclude that the people in question were not believers at all. He must have been writing about non-believers who became interested in Christianity but didn't continue. After all, what about 'Once saved, always saved'? But the description in chapter 6 of the people who are in danger is surely a description of those who have been born again! The writer is talking to those who have been 'enlightened', who have 'tasted the heavenly gift', who have 'shared in the Holy Spirit', who have 'tasted the goodness of the word of God and the powers of the coming age'. I cannot fit any unbeliever into that description. In any other letter, these phrases would not even be questioned as a description of Christians.

There is a passage in 1 Peter which uses almost identical language to describe Christians: 'Like newborn babes, crave pure spiritual milk so that by it you may grow up in your salvation, now that you have tasted that the Lord is good.' This is clearly about believers, yet it is using similar language to Hebrews chapter 6. The whole of 1 Peter is addressed to believers. Even calling them 'spiritual infants' implies that they have been born again.

The warnings given involve two phases. Phase 1 is neglecting the faith and drifting away. Phase 2 is denying the faith. There is a difference, therefore, between Phase 1 (what is known as backsliding) and Phase 2 (what is called apostasy).

Backsliding is a recoverable condition, but according to Hebrews 6 we can get to a point of no return where there is no possibility of recovering our salvation. So Hebrews 6 doesn't discuss whether you can lose your salvation, but whether having lost it, you can find it again. The answer is that you can't.

We must warn those who are backsliding and drifting of the danger they are in, because there can come a point where they can't find their way back. I wish Hebrews didn't say that! But I cannot get round chapter 6 and other parts of the epistle, which are so urgent in their pleading from beginning to end. This terrible danger looms down the road for those who 'pull up their anchor', 'lower their sails' and 'drift away'.

Some suggest that these are hypothetical warnings – that this severe danger could never happen. But this argument does not hold. I believe there is hypocrisy in threatening people with something that could never happen. The Bible is the word of truth, not a book that plays games with people. Hebrews alone convinces me that it is possible to reach a point of no return in drifting away from Jesus, even without other passages in other New Testament books. The ultimate point of apostasy for these Hebrews believers would be standing in front of the synagogue and denying that Jesus is the Messiah. In so doing they would be crucifying Jesus afresh. The writer warns that if you crucify him afresh, he can do you no more good, which is a solemn warning.

It's important to add that this doesn't mean that believers should wake up every morning wondering if they are saved or not. There is an assurance in the New Testament that comes from a believer's walk with the Lord. Assurance in the New Testament is not based on a decision made at a point in time, but on one's present relationship with God. Paul reminds us in his Letter to the Romans that the Spirit goes on witnessing with the believer's spirit that he or she is a child of God (Romans 8:16; cf. 1 John 4:13).

To put it another way, you can have a present assurance that you are on the way to heaven, but I don't believe there are any guarantees that you will get there. So if you keep on that way and keep on believing in Jesus, you are certain to arrive. The teaching of Hebrews does not produce neurotic Christians wondering whether they are saved or not, but it does produce serious Christians who don't play games with God, who don't backslide and who don't neglect their faith and drift away.

Throughout the New Testament there are some very solemn warnings to Christians about backsliding. In John 15 Jesus says, 'I am the vine; you are the branches. If a man remains in me and I in him, he will bear much fruit.' But then he says, 'If anyone does not remain in me, he is like a branch that is thrown away and withers; such branches are picked up, thrown into the fire and burned.' I can't twist that! Common sense tells you what it says.

It is interesting that the failure of over two million of the Jews who had left Egypt to make it to Canaan is used by three different New Testament writers as a warning to Christians that they might have started well in their Christian lives, but they need to make sure they arrive. We may have left Egypt, but we need to make it to Canaan. This is used by Paul in 1 Corinthians 10, by the writer of Hebrews in chapter 4 of his letter and by Jude as a warning to Christians. It is not those who start but those who finish who make it.

I remember seeing Billy Graham being interviewed on television. The interviewer asked him a question he had not been asked before: 'What will be your first thought when you get to heaven?' Billy immediately replied, 'Relief! Relief that I made it.' Now there is a humble man who isn't cocksure, but knows he is on the way. I am sure right now that I am on the way to heaven – the Spirit tells me I am on the right road. But I can't tell you more than that. I intend to keep on travelling till I make it.

John Bunyan's *Pilgrim's Progress* pictures the Christian life as a journey, from the sinful city to the celestial city. At the end, the main character 'Christian' and his companion face the crossing of the River Jordan – the dark, deep, black river of death. They don't like it one bit. Christian's companion says he is unwilling to go through that river, and turns off to the left down a side path, hoping for another way over. Bunyan writes, 'So I saw in my dream that there is a way to hell, even from the gates of heaven.' The companion had been on the right path, but he left it just before he arrived at the celestial city.

This theme is also clear in the Book of Revelation. The whole book is a message for people under terrific pressure. The promise to those who overcome is that God will not blot out their names from the Lamb's Book of Life. What does that mean? If you want to keep your name in the Book of Life, then overcome, go right on to the end, never go back, keep your eyes fixed on Jesus. There is a warning on the last page of the Bible that if you play around with the Book of Revelation and start taking things out of it or adding things to it, God will take away your share in the tree of life.

So, you see, there is this thread of warning alongside the glorious scriptures which tell us of God's keeping power. If you have the Father, Son and Holy Spirit on your side, you have got everything going for you. Just keep on believing, and you will make it.

Conclusions

1. It is possible for us to 'lose our salvation'

The book is a warning to us all that we should continue trusting and not think that a one-off decision for Christ will necessarily mean that we will be saved on the final day. (See also my book, *Once Saved, Always Saved?*, Hodder & Stoughton, 1996.)

2. Once you are lost it is impossible to recover

This is the message of Hebrews 6. Such teaching is found elsewhere, notably in 1 John 5:16. It is a solemn message, but I don't believe we can interpret these scriptures any other way.

3. Predestination requires our continued co-operation

It is not automatic. God did predestine us. He chose us before we chose him, but he requires our co-operation. It is as if someone threw a rope to a drowning man, and the man throwing the rope said, 'Grab hold of this, and hold on until I have got you to the shore.' Would the drowning man say, when he got to the shore, that he had saved himself by hanging on? Never! He would say that someone had saved him. The idea that you saved yourself because you held on is just not true, but you have your part to play. That is why Peter, in his Second Letter, urges his readers to make their calling and election sure (2 Peter 1:10–11). God has elected us and chosen us, so we make that sure by pressing on, by going on for maturity, so that we may have a rich welcome into heaven.

I believe in predestination. God predestined me to be his son; God elected me, chose me; he was after me long before I was after him. But I need to make that calling and election sure by holding on to the rope until I am safely on the shore.

So I want to be both a Calvinist and an Arminian. These

two schools of thought have tended to be set in opposition to each other, Calvinists stressing the electing work of God, among other things, and Arminians stressing our need to persevere.

Hebrews is the one book that I don't think we can twist on this issue and say it is full of problems. It is full of clear statements that we need to hear.

4. Holiness is as necessary as forgiveness

We have seen that it is not just those who accept the forgiveness of God who make it, but those who press on. This implies that holiness is as necessary as forgiveness. It is no good claiming to be forgiven if we are not prepared to acknowledge the lordship of Christ and live a godly life. The verse in Hebrews which encapsulates this teaching is 12:14: 'Make every effort to live in peace with all men and to be holy; without holiness no-one will see the Lord.' I find that far too many Christians today want forgiveness but not holiness; they want happiness from Jesus in this life and holiness in the next. But the will of God in my New Testament is clearly holiness in this life, even if it makes me unhappy. Our hedonistic generation just wants pleasure, not pain.

Hebrews 12:7 says God is prepared to chastise us, to cause us pain, if that will make us more holy. The one thing he is after is our holiness, and he can make it tough for his children. Hebrews even goes so far as to say that if the Lord has never chastised you, you are a bastard and not a true son. The full gospel is that forgiveness and holiness are both gifts of grace. They are both offered on the same basis – faith. But you need both.

5. God is a holy God

Following the publication of my book *The Road to Hell* (Hodder & Stoughton, 1992), in which I outlined the Bible's teaching on hell, I had a number of BBC radio interviews. Every interviewer asked the same question: 'How can a loving God send anyone to hell?' What interests me is that no one ever asks, 'How can a holy God send anyone to hell?' Yet God is holy, and his love is holy love, which means he will never be content with less than holiness for the ones he loves. Hebrews emphasizes this point repeatedly. Note the following passages:

■ Without the shedding of blood there is no forgiveness (9:22).
■ Without faith it is impossible to please God (11:6).
■ It is a dreadful thing to fall into the hands of the living God (10:31).
■ Let us be thankful, and so worship God acceptably with reverence and awe, for our God is a consuming fire (12:28).

What value does Hebrews have for believers?

1 It aids our Bible study. It helps us to understand the relationship between the Old and New Testaments. The shadow concept is most helpful for understanding the Old Testament; we can note the ways in which hints of Jesus are found there.

2 It is Christ-centred and so helps to keep our eyes fixed on Jesus. The writer constantly makes Jesus his focus. In particular, it is the only New Testament book to major on his priesthood. His present work in heaven is to intercede for us. Some have even called Hebrews the 'Fifth Gospel' because of its emphasis on Christ.

3 It is faith-building. It is an inspiration to think of the many
   people who have gone before us and who are watching us
   (see especially chapter 11).

4 It warns us of the danger of backsliding. We are given
   severe warnings about the two stages: the drifting away,
   whereby we stop meeting with other believers and neglect
   our faith; and the deliberate, wilful apostasy whereby we
   deny our faith in Christ altogether.

5 It emphasizes the importance of church membership. It
   stresses that safety lies in fellowship when we are under
   pressure. The devil will pick off Christians on their own.
   So when the pressure is on, stay close to the family. The
   book urges the readers to remember their leaders (13:7)
   and to co-operate with them. It also reminds them of the
   need to keep on loving, visiting those in prison and
   spurring one another on towards good deeds.

6 It helps in times of persecution. The book also reminds us
   of the way the believers were treated in the early days of
   persecution at the hands of Nero. In view of such threats
   and difficulties, it is important to stay focused on Christ.
   Such passages are especially valuable to believers facing
   persecution today.

PART II

JAMES

Introduction

There are two particular difficulties in studying Scripture. One is mental difficulty, when you don't understand what you are reading, and the other is moral difficulty, when you do understand it! More people have moral difficulties than mental difficulties, and if ever a book is likely to give the former, it is James. It is a frightening book, because once you have read it, you can't plead ignorance. It is one of the easiest books in the Bible to understand and the hardest to undertake.

How practical!

Most people's first impression of the book is that it is extremely practical. This is no-nonsense Christianity for daily life – where the rubber hits the road. It is realistic, with very little focus on doctrine and an awful lot on duty.

On my bookshelf at home I have a number of commentaries on James, all with 'action' titles: *Truth in Action, Faith that Works, Behaviour of Belief, Belief that Behaves, Make Your Faith Work*. They all emphasize that the key word of the Letter of James is 'do' – a word that is also important in the rest of the Bible. Unfortunately we tend to overlook the little words, preferring to just underline theological terms like 'justification' and 'sanctification', but the word 'do' is also common in the Bible and just as important.

In Matthew's Gospel there is a short parable about the father who told his two sons to work in his vineyard. One said no initially, but went nevertheless. The other said yes, but never arrived. Jesus asks which of the two *did* the father's will, not which of the two *said* the right thing. It was the doing that was important.

It is the same in James. We have this challenge to be 'doers of the word' and not just hearers of it.

How illogical!

As well as seeming simple, the book also seems illogical. It's full of practical counsel that can't be put into order. I tried to make a diagram of James and failed totally. I even tried to get a structured outline, but was unable to do so because of the way he wanders around from one subject to another. He starts a subject, then he leaves it, then he comes back to it later. They are pearls of wisdom that haven't been strung. Yet in some ways this serves the purpose of the book, for it is a book urging us to action rather than analysis.

The practical and illogical elements added together give strong reminders of the Book of Proverbs in the Old Testament. It too has little structure and focuses on the day-to-day issues in life. This is what is known as Jewish wisdom literature. The Rabbis have different forms of preaching, but there is one form where they simply 'muse aloud'. It is called *charaz*. There is no prepared address, but just an elderly Rabbi in the synagogue sharing pearls and gems of wisdom.

James was clearly taught by such a Rabbi when he was a young man, because he is a master of *charaz*, and he is just doing the same thing for his readers.

Who is James?

There are five people called James in the New Testament. Perhaps the best known is James the son of Zebedee and the brother of John, who was the first martyred apostle, beheaded by Herod in AD 44. Next there is James the son of Alphaeus, another of the Twelve. There is James the father of Judas (not Iscariot). There is James the little (mentioned in Mark 15:40). Finally, there is James the half-brother of Jesus. It was this final James who penned the epistle.

James was one of four half-brothers of Jesus who, together with a number of sisters (we don't know how many), formed the family circle. Few realize that at least five, and possibly seven, of the twelve apostles were Jesus' cousins, which explains why so many of them were present at a private wedding at Cana in Galilee (see John chapter 2). The disciples would not have just turned up uninvited.

So Jesus found quite a number of apostles from his wider family circle. But his immediate family didn't know what to make of him. When you have lived with someone for 30 years and they suddenly go around saying they are the Messiah, it can't be easy! At the beginning of his public ministry he seems to disown Mary (most assume that Joseph had died by this time). He didn't call her 'mother' any more – he called her 'woman'. 'Woman, what have I to do with you?' was his first recorded comment to Mary, at the wedding at Cana.

Furthermore, there was clearly tension between Jesus and the rest of the family. At one time his family came to take him home and lock him away, because they thought he was out of his mind (Mark 3:21). Finding a large crowd surrounding him, they sent a message through to Jesus: 'Your mother and brother and sisters have come to take you home.' He replied, 'My mother – who is my mother? My brothers and sisters – who are my brothers and sisters? Anybody who does the will of my Father in heaven is my mother, my brother and my sister.' His family thought this was crazy talk, and no doubt Mary felt hurt by the implications.

It seems that Jesus almost dissociated himself from his mother until the cross, where he said to John, 'That is your mother' – in effect asking John to be Mary's son in his place. Apart from her being mentioned as one of those who were at the prayer meeting before the day of Pentecost, that is the last we hear of Mary in the Gospels. You never hear her name again. She had played her role, and it was now over. She was a remarkable woman. I am happy to call her 'blessed', because she prophesied that all generations would call her blessed. I am not prepared to call her a virgin now, because she had other children after Jesus by Joseph (Mark 6:3).

Things were not smooth between Jesus and his brothers. In John 7:3–5 the brothers reminded him that it was the time of the Feast of Tabernacles, and teased him that he really ought to go, because the Jews expected the Messiah to come at that Feast. What an ideal time to declare himself!

Yet in spite of this suspicion and disdain, two of these brothers became writers of the New Testament – Jude and James. It is said that when Jesus died on the cross, his brother James was so deeply upset and full of regret about what he had said about him and how he had teased him, that he said he would never eat food again. He would have fasted until he died, except that three days later Jesus appeared to his followers and to James personally. From that moment on, James called himself a bond-slave of Jesus.

Although these two brothers wrote two books of the New Testament, they never took advantage of their relationship to Jesus. They never said, 'Listen to me – I am a brother of Jesus.' Jude actually says, 'I am the brother of James.' So his own brothers were persuaded by the resurrection that Jesus, who had lived with them in the carpenter's cottage in Nazareth, was none other than the Son of God. James is mentioned as a member of the little prayer group that waited for the coming of the Spirit at Pentecost. So Jesus' cousins followed him, and his immediate family believed in him. That tells you something about the quality of Jesus' character.

The next mention of James comes in Acts 15, where he is the presiding elder of the fellowship in Jerusalem. He wasn't one of the Twelve, and yet clearly by unanimous consent, he was recognized as the leader of the mother church in Jerusalem.

His role in Acts 15 was especially crucial. He faced a most difficult and delicate crisis – the biggest in the early church's life. It concerned the whole question of circumcision, and whether Christianity would remain a Jewish sect or would become a universal faith. James presided over the meeting that could have split the church right down the middle if agreement had not been reached. But James saved it by appealing to the Spirit and to the Scriptures. Peter reported what the Spirit had done with Cornelius and his household, and then James said, 'Well, that ties in with what Scripture says', and quoted from the Old Testament. It is important to note that rather than giving his flock a command – since, as Christians, they were not under the Law – he encouraged them to choose a loving response to this issue.

If there is one thing I long to see, it is people who understand the Spirit and people who know the Scriptures getting together. We are in danger of diverging. I have been part of the charismatic renewal in this country, but my greatest concern is that it is drifting away from its scriptural bearings.

I have an equal concern for those who know the Scriptures inside out, but don't know the dynamic of the Holy Spirit.

I have written about this theme in *Word and Spirit Together* (Hodder & Stoughton, 1993).

So on the basis of this understanding from the Spirit and the word, James gave a judgement upon which everybody agreed. What could have been a catastrophe turned into a beautifully uniting moment, under James.

After this council, a letter was sent out to the Gentile believers everywhere, which explained that the Gentiles should not have any burden from the Law of Moses, but should be sensitive to the scruples of Jewish Christians when eating with them. The letter promoted a position similar to that set out by Paul in Romans concerning disagreement among Christians over issues not directly dealt with in Scripture. Paul said that those who have liberty in disputable matters must be prepared to forgo their liberty for the sake of the weaker brother. It is true, of course, that the more you mature in the Christian faith, the freer you are from scruples, but while a person still has them, more mature believers should give way.

Scruples can be very awkward. Often we feel guilty about doing something because we were told as a child that it was wrong. I was taught as a child that we shouldn't ride bicycles or use cameras on a Sunday. Well, it was years before I found out that there was no verse in the Bible about cameras and bicycles! When I worked on a farm I had to cycle five miles to get to church, and it was such a strange position feeling guilty about cycling to worship God! But as you grow up in Christ, you feel more and more free to enjoy things that God has freely given you.

Others may feel awkward about certain practices which are all right in themselves but which would be a stumbling-block because of their association with the person's pre-Christian past. The classic example is drinking wine at a meal with a former alcoholic. If you know that someone would find this a problem, it is loving to forgo your liberty for the sake of the Christian brother or sister's conscience. If I am with a Jew, I stick to a kosher food diet, just as the apostle Paul did. We need to be adaptable and sensitive to other people's consciences and not flaunt our own freedom.

When James sent this letter from Jerusalem to the Gentile believers, he also wrote another letter to go to the Jewish believers, and this is the Letter of James. It is a letter telling the Jews how to behave in the Gentile world. The advice corresponds almost exactly with the letter in Acts 15 to the Gentiles about how to behave towards the Jewish world. So it is a mirror reflection of that letter, albeit a much longer one.

Other historical documents tell us that James stayed in Jerusalem and was given the nickname 'James the Just', which was a wonderful quality for a presiding elder. He also had a second nickname, 'Oblias', which means a bulwark, a really reliable person.

James came to a tragic but glorious end. Following the death of Festus, the Roman Governor, and before Albinius took up office, there was a gap of about two months in AD 62 when there was no Roman Governor. The Jewish rulers seized the opportunity to attack Christians, because there was no Roman government to say, 'You can't put anyone to death.' At that time they captured him, took him to the pinnacle of the temple and said, 'Now blaspheme Christ, or we will throw you off!' This was the very pinnacle where the devil took Jesus in Matthew chapter 4. James the Just simply replied: 'I see the Son of Man coming on the clouds of glory!' So they threw him off.

But the fall didn't kill him, so they started to stone him. As he lay there, with his bones broken and the stones being thrown at him, he said, 'Father, forgive them, for they don't know what they do.' The crowd watching cried out, 'James the Just is praying for us!' What an end! Finally someone, out of sheer mercy, got a big wooden club and clubbed his head, and he died. Of course, he was only one of the many who perished for Jesus in those early years.

When his fellow Christians came to pick up his body and give him a decent burial, they were astonished, because for the first time they saw his knees, which looked like the knees of a camel. Here was a man who spent more time on his knees than on his feet!

He was well regarded within the church. Eusebius, one of the early church fathers, said of him:

> *The philosophy and godliness which his life displayed to so eminent a degree, was the occasion of a universal belief in him as the 'most just of men'.*

Hence the nickname, James the Just. One of the writers at the time, Hegessipus, said:

> *James was a Nazirite. He was in the habit of entering alone into the temple, and was frequently found upon his knees begging forgiveness for the people, so that his knees became hard like a camel, in consequence of his constantly bending them in his worship of God, and asking forgiveness for the people. Because of his exceeding great justice he was called 'the just'.*

Authorship

James was so well known that further identification at the start of his letter was unnecessary – 'James' was sufficient. Interestingly, he includes a number of Jesus' sayings from the Sermon on the Mount (23 quotations). As far as we know, James wasn't there to hear them, so he must have picked them up either directly from Jesus, or later from the Twelve as the collection of Jesus' sayings circulated.

However, in spite of the historical evidence linking James with this letter, doubt has been cast upon his authorship, because the style of the letter is so unlike what might be expected from a Galilean. Other Jews despised the Galileans in part because of their distinctive dialect. They were regarded as illiterate. In Acts the Chief Priest reflects on the courage of the apostles: 'How can these uneducated men challenge us like this?' But the Greek style in which the letter is written is much more polished than might be expected.

Style

James uses a number of the best devices of public speaking. Let me run through them.

1 He uses rhetorical questions – that is, questions that don't require an answer but make the hearer think. See 2:4–5, 14–16; 3:11–12; 4:4, 12.

2 He uses paradoxical statements to gain attention. For example: 'Count it all joy, my brothers, when you face trials of various kinds' (1:2). 'Joy' and 'trials' don't seem to go together, so this gains attention. See also the irony in 2:14–19; 5:5.

3 He has imaginary conversations in which he creates a dialogue with someone. Once again this raises people's interest levels. People are always fascinated to overhear conversations. See 2:18; 5:13.

4 He also uses questions to introduce new subjects. See 2:14; 4:1.

5 He includes many imperatives in the letter – there are 60 of them in just 108 verses!

6 He personifies things. He talks of sin as if it is an animal, and he uses pictures and figures from everyday life. He talks about ships' rudders, forest fires, and bridles and

horses in a farmer's life, all of which gain attention.

7 He uses famous men and women such as Elijah, Abraham and Rahab as examples.

8 He particularly uses a direct form of address – 'you' – which is a great way of getting attention.

9 He is not afraid to use harsh language. See 2:20; 4:4.

10 He sometimes uses vivid antithesis (contrasting opposites). See 2:13, 26.

11 He often uses quotations. See 1:11, 17; 4:6; 5:11, 20.

So how did such speaking devices find their way into the letter? I think the answer lies in what we find in 1 Peter 2. Many of the writers of the New Testament didn't actually write but dictated the text. They used an amanuensis – what we would call a shorthand typist or a secretary today.

Both Paul and Peter, for example, used Silas quite a lot in this capacity. So it looks as if James delivered all this verbally, and got someone to write it down for him, knock it into shape and send it off as a circular letter. This explanation would solve all the 'problems' that some scholars have. So we have got Greek rhetoric and Hebrew wisdom combined in this letter.

The readers

The letter is not addressed to a church, or a group of churches, or an individual, like most of the New Testament letters. It is addressed to the 12 tribes scattered among the nations, which makes it quite clear that it is addressed to the Jewish Dispersion – to the churches started among the dispersed Jews around the Mediterranean. It mentions the Lord Jesus Christ in the first verse, and 'my brothers' on 12 occasions.

The Jews were dispersed twice: once to Babylon in the involuntary exile of 586 BC, and again just before Jesus came, when many opted to settle all over the Mediterranean world.

There were more Jews outside than inside Israel, with as many as 10,000 Jews in Rome itself. Many would return three times a year for the Jewish festivals, but they quickly imbibed the culture around them, so much so that the Jews became a byword for hypocrisy.

So Christ came at the ideal time for the spread of the gospel. The Jews had been scattered around the Mediterranean, the Roman roads had been built and the Greek language was spoken everywhere – it was absolutely perfect. God had prepared the whole situation for the rapid spread of the news about Jesus. When the apostle Paul arrived in a new place on his missionary journeys, he went first to the synagogue, believing that the first converts would be from the God-fearing people there.

It is clear that the Jewish Christians in the Dispersion around the Mediterranean faced a totally different situation to the Jewish believers at home. The Jerusalem church was made up almost entirely of Jewish believers. They were isolated and segregated, and so became too strict. Legalism and the pride that goes with it were their biggest problems. But in the Dispersion, the Jewish believers faced the problem of assimilation. Many were embarrassed to be known as Christians and were too lax in their behaviour. Their problem was greed, because most of them had left Israel for business reasons in search of riches elsewhere. They were becoming too much like the Gentiles.

Content

Wealth

Our introduction has touched on a number of themes picked up by James, with business being one of the major ones. It is a key concern for any Jew. They have been hounded from one country to another, so they have needed a trade or profession that is easily portable. That is why so many of them have become tailors, for they only need to take a needle and thread with them, and they are in business. Others have become jewellers, because a jeweller's goods can be easily packed into a small suitcase. They have also become moneylenders, of course. In medieval Europe Christians were not allowed to be moneylenders, so the Jews became bankers, with the Rothschilds among the most famous.

But the focus on business has its own snags. Jesus said, 'You cannot worship God and money' – you can't devote yourself to God and to money-making at the same time. The Pharisees laughed when Jesus said that, because they were both rich and religious. But Jesus said, 'It is impossible.' They said, 'He doesn't know how to make money, so he is just against the rich.' But Jesus constantly warned us that it is hard for rich people to get into the Kingdom – and, of course, by New Testament standards, most Western Christians are rich. Money itself is neutral and can do a lot of good. But Paul writes, 'The *love* of money is the root of *all kinds* of evil.'

It is clear from the Letter of James that wealth had corrupted some of his readers. They were exploiting their employees, holding back their wages to help the cash-flow of the business. They were indulging themselves, spending their money on needless luxuries. They were flattering the rich people who came into their assemblies, telling the poor people to sit at the back, but showing the rich people to the front seats. Others were insulting and despising poor people.

It is the same the world over – when you make money, you regard yourself as successful, and others as failures who haven't made it. Snobbery goes with wealth.

This attitude prevails in some churches today, where the few rich people in the fellowship effectively control what happens. Staff are reluctant to be unpopular, for fear of angering major donors who have an unhealthy authority.

Being wealthy actually gave false security. Godliness is life lived in reference to God. Money wreaks havoc with godliness, because when you have got plenty of money, you make plans without reference to God. James said they should always add 'God willing' to any plans that were made. My father always used to put 'D.V.' (*Deo volente* – Latin for 'God willing') in his letters to acknowedge that any plans he made were made in reference to God. James preached against the wealthy who left out the 'D.V.'

The neglect of God and the neglect of the poor tend to accompany money-making. James lists other sins common to the rich: envy, because the more you have, the more you want, and the more you envy those who have got more; selfish ambition; pride; boasting and bragging; presumption; impatience; anger; covetousness; arguments; quarrels; fights and litigation. Litigation is one of the pastimes of the rich. You could take the Letter of James into the City of London and preach on it.

I was once asked to go and speak to the members of the Stock Exchange. They asked me for a sermon title before I went, and so I told them it would be 'You can't take it with you, and if you did it would burn'. They absolutely refused to publicize the title! So I changed it to 'How to invest beyond the grave', and they were quite interested!

The tongue

James also focuses on the tongue as a major cause of problems for the believer. We might speculate that he could recall his own idle words when teasing Jesus (in John chapter 7).

The Jews love words, but there was an inherent danger in speaking too much. A particular weakness for expatriates was gossip. People far from home gossip within their little community. James understands this only too well, and he has a lot to say about the tongue and words.

He says things such as, 'You use the same tongue to bless people and curse them. It is like bitter and sweet water coming out of the same fountain.' James says that the tongue is the hardest part of your body to control. If you can control it, you are perfect. So the tongue is a ready reckoner for how holy you are. Consider your speech, because it is 'out of the abundance of the heart that your mouth speaks.' You are entirely sanctified when you always say the right thing, when you keep silent when you should, and when you speak up when you should. Jesus said we shall be judged on the Day of Judgement for 'every careless word', because it is the careless words, spoken when you are tired or busy, that reveal your real heart, not your careful speech, when you are thinking about what to say.

Other images are used to describe the tongue: it has been set on fire by hell; it is like a little ship's rudder, and it can turn the whole ship. The effects are like a forest fire that was started with just one match. Sins of the tongue, such as grumbling, cursing, lying and swearing, are all mentioned in this little letter.

Important though the themes of wealth and words are, the two words that open up the letter are 'world' and 'wisdom'.

The world

James explains that 'friendship with the world is enmity with God' – you can't be popular with the world and with God. Jesus wasn't, and if he couldn't manage it, neither will we. In fact, the apostle Paul taught that the godlier we are, the less popular we are likely to be. Paul actually said to Timothy,

'Whoever would live a godly life in Christ Jesus will suffer persecution.' Non-believers may respect you, but they will try to knock your faith out of you.

James said that 'pure religion before God' meant two things: 'to keep yourself untainted from the world and to visit widows and orphans in their distress'.

It is often said that Christians should be 'in the world but not of it'. This is true, but it does not mean that we should stay away from non-believers. When my good friend Peter was a car dealer in Australia, he would sack any member of his staff who became a Christian. (Don't worry – he found them a job elsewhere first!) He did so on the principle that he couldn't be a witness at work if he was surrounded by Christians!

James teaches us the difference between being tested and being tempted. God will never tempt us, but he will test us. The difference is this: you test people in the hope that they will pass the test, but you tempt them hoping they will fail. God will test you, so we should count it all joy when things get tough, for we know God is moving us up a class. It is the devil who tempts us and wants us to fail. However, he can only tempt us if there is something in us that he can use to make us want to take the bait. But God has promised us that we will never be tempted more than we can cope with – which means, of course, that the devil is totally under God's control. The devil can't touch us unless he gets permission from God first. (See the early chapters of Job for a prime example of this.)

So you will never, ever be able to say as a Christian, 'I couldn't help it.' So in the world we face testing and temptation. One comes from God in the hope that you will pass the test; the other comes from the devil in the hope that you will fail. We need the wisdom to discern which is which. When the missionary Hudson Taylor's wife suffered greatly towards the end of her life, and became totally blind, somebody asked: 'Why should God do this to you when you have served him so faithfully?' 'Oh,' she said, 'he is putting the finishing touches to my character.'

So life won't get easier as we get older. I find that guidance gets harder. In the early years of being a Christian, God has mercy on us, giving us such clear guidance that we have no doubt about what we should be doing. But then he puts us in a situation where we have really got to begin to work things out for ourselves. He doesn't spoon-feed us as we mature, but gives us more responsibility, and trusts us to make judgements instead of giving us a clear line.

Wisdom

We noted earlier the similarity between James and Proverbs, so it is no surprise to learn that wisdom is another key theme of the letter. James isolates two categories of wisdom. Just as there are two sorts of trial – testing and temptation – so there are two sorts of wisdom – wisdom from above and wisdom from below.

The wisdom from below comes from human experience through having tried things out – we call it the school of experience. But there is another way to get wisdom, which doesn't take so long. We simply ask for it! James says that if anyone lacks wisdom, they shouldn't assume that they must stay that way. He explains that wisdom comes by asking God, without double-mindedness and without doubting.

Wisdom is far more available than we realize. James says it is a lovely wisdom because it is pure and it is peaceable – it solves the problem. All divine wisdom is available to you at any moment. When you are in difficulty, all you have got to say is, 'Lord, I need wisdom.' And you will be astonished at the response.

Problems

We need to look now at the so-called 'problems' posed by the Letter of James.

Its general tone

It doesn't seem to be a very Christian letter. There is not much about Christ or the gospel in it. There seems to be more emphasis on man's activity than God's, on deeds rather than doctrine, on law rather than gospel, on works rather than faith. It does not mention key events, such as Jesus' death, resurrection and ascension, or the ministry of the Holy Spirit. It seems to be about doing good deeds.

So some have questioned whether the book describes Christianity as it is found in the rest of the Bible. Notable thinkers have written it off. The Protestant reformer Martin Luther said he was disgusted with the letter, that it contained nothing evangelical and failed to show Christ. (In fact Christ is only mentioned twice in the whole letter.) Luther called it a 'right strawy epistle', meaning that there is no corn in it, just straw, which is just about as insulting a remark as you can make. He said, 'I do not believe it is apostolic. It would be better not to have it in the New Testament.' When he translated the Bible, he put James in an appendix at the end, together with Hebrews, Jude and Revelation. He didn't quite have the courage to cut it right out, but he shifted it out of the main text.

Indeed, there is very little in this whole letter that an orthodox Jew couldn't accept. It talks of the Law, the synagogue, brothers and elders, and addresses God as 'God Almighty'. If you were to remove the two mentions of Christ, and the words 'born', 'name', 'coming' and 'believers', an orthodox Jew would agree with everything.

Its specific teaching

In addition to these problems, there is a more specific concern, which has caused great consternation among Bible readers. In 2:24 James says, 'You see that a person is justified by what he does and not by faith alone.' This seems to undermine the teaching of the New Testament, and of the apostle Paul in particular, about how we can be right with God. Luther said it undermined the fundamental gospel truth of 'justification by faith alone'.

The general tone of the letter and the specific concern about its teaching on faith meant that it had a hard fight to get into the New Testament and a hard fight to stay there. It was one of the last letters to be included (in AD 350).

So how do we deal with this apparent contradiction? A number of points can be made:

1 James died in AD 62 and so couldn't have read Paul's letters on the subject, though he knew Paul and persuaded him to observe the Nazirite law to show he was still Jewish (see Acts 21:18–25). So if there is a contradiction, it can't be deliberate.

2 Paul was writing for Gentiles, whereas James was writing for Jewish believers, so their purpose was different. Paul was defending Gentiles from Jewish legalism, while James was defending Jews from Gentile licence. It is not surprising, therefore, that there is a difference in emphasis.

3 When we come to the specific 'problem' passage, we find that the word 'works' has several different meanings. Paul writes of the works of the Law, while James writes of the works of faith – that is, *actions*. What James is saying is, 'Faith without actions is dead.' He is not commenting on the works of the Law. He uses an illustration to show that love without actions is no use. Suppose someone says to a

brother, 'Oh my, you don't have any clothes or food, do you? Well, God bless you, brother, God bless you!' James asks, 'What use is that?' That is love without action, love without the works of love.

So when he talks about faith, he is talking about faith without action. And unless you act in faith, you don't have faith. Professing faith can't save you. Faith must be practised. He says even the devils believe in God, and they tremble!

But then he gives an illustration of faith with action, using Abraham and Rahab, a good man and a bad woman. They both acted in faith, one prepared to take life and the other to save it. Abraham acted in faith when he prepared to kill his son, his only hope of descendants. Rahab the prostitute acted in faith when she looked after the spies and asked them to save her from the coming invasion.

James is saying that faith is not something you profess. You have got to show you believe in Jesus by acting. You will fall flat on your face if he doesn't catch you. That is faith. So James is absolutely right when he says faith without actions cannot save you, for such faith is as dead as a corpse. Faith is not reciting the Creed, it is acting in faith, demonstrating trust in the Lord.

So with Paul and James, God is giving us two different angles on this crucial issue so that we get it in balance and get the whole truth. Legalism says we are saved by works; licence says we are saved without works; but liberty (the Christian position) says we are saved for works, but they are good works, works of love.

Even Paul, the apparent champion of justification by faith, says in Ephesians 2: 'For we are God's workmanship, created in Christ Jesus to do good works, which God prepared in advance for us to do.' So we are not saved by good deeds, but we are saved for good deeds, and we will be judged by our deeds.

James, the apparent champion of works, says in 2:5 that believers should be 'rich in faith'.

Legalism says, 'We are going to make sure that you are not free to sin, by making rules and regulations.' Licence says, 'We are free to sin.' Liberty says, 'We are free not to sin.' These may sound like neat clichés, but nevertheless they are true. It is the most important thing in the Christian life to get a clear grasp of the differences between those three statements, because this is the heart of the gospel, and we need both Paul and James to get this right. So on the general question of 'faith versus works', I believe that the Letter of James needs the rest of the New Testament, and the rest of the New Testament needs James.

In his assessment of the letter, Martin Luther completely missed the point. He said it contradicts Paul and all the other Scriptures, but Luther was no more infallible than the Pope he opposed. He was too focused on the doctrine of justification by faith to see how important James' emphasis really was. Faith must act and be worked out. What God has worked in has to be worked out in the world, in an alien atmosphere.

Conclusion

We are not dispersed Jews, so is the letter relevant to us? It is very relevant to us, because we are dispersed Christians. Some Christians are so wrapped up in church life that they are more like the Jews in Jerusalem. Their problem is pride, caused in part by being isolated from the world.

But most Christians are like the Jews in the Dispersion, working in the everyday world, tempted to become assimilated into the world and to adopt its moral standards. We are citizens of heaven but strangers on earth, part of the dispersed people of God, awaiting our future dwelling where we will be finally home. We are in the world but not of it.

Our position is best summed up by the Epistle to Diognetus, written at the end of the first century AD. The Epistle is a response to the question: 'What's different about the Christians?' He said:

> *Christians are distinguished from other men neither by country nor language. Living in such places as the lot of each has determined and following the customs of the natives in respect to clothing, food and the rest of their ordinary conduct, they display their wonderful and confessedly striking method of life. They dwell in their own countries, but simply as sojourners. As citizens, they share in all things with others, and yet endure all things as foreigners. Every foreign land is to them as their native country, and every land of their birth as a land of strangers. They pass their days on earth, but they are citizens of heaven. They obey the prescribed laws, and at the same time, surpass the laws by their lives. They are reviled and they bless ...*

Christians today need to live in that fashion – to make sure that the world remains external to them. The world's motives, methods and morals are still a challenge. The pressures on Christians today remain essentially the same as they were back in the first century. In this regard, the Letter of James is right up to date and of great value to any believer seeking to follow Christ. It focuses on how to behave in the world and in the church. James is particularly interested in what we do, not what we say. Bible knowledge is useless unless we do something about it.

PART III

1 AND 2 PETER

1 Peter

On 2 September 1666 there was a great fire in London. It began in a baker's oven and caused tremendous damage. Two hundred thousand people lost their homes, since most of the houses were timber-framed and so were unable to withstand the flames. It was estimated that the fire did £10 million worth of damage. Altogether 90 churches were destroyed, although many of them were later rebuilt by Christopher Wren, including St Paul's Cathedral. Of course, when there is a disaster, it is one of the unfortunate sides of human nature that people look round for a scapegoat. Often the innocent are accused, and in the case of the great fire of London, the French Catholics were blamed.

On 19 July AD 64 a fire began in the city of Rome which lasted for three days, devastating much of the city. It engulfed the centre of Rome, destroying temples and houses. The citizens looked for a scapegoat, and found one in the Emperor Nero. They knew he had ambitions to pull down old buildings and put up new magnificent structures, so they assumed he was behind it. Nero, in turn, shifted the blame onto the Christians, and so began a serious persecution of the church.

They faced awful times. They were tortured, sewn into the skins of wild beasts and made to crawl round the amphitheatres on all fours, while they were set upon by lions and other wild animals. They were hunted by dogs and some of them were crucified.

I remember standing with my back to the Colosseum in Rome and looking at a low, green hill which used to be Nero's palace garden. I thought of the day when he held a barbecue in that garden. He had some Christians coated with tar and bitumen, tied them to posts around the garden and set them on fire. They were burned alive to provide lighting for his party.

The news of this barbarism against God's people spread through the whole Roman Empire from church to church. But as the news spread, so too did a letter from the apostle Peter. He wrote it to the Christians with whom he had a special connection and interest in what we now call north-west Turkey, to warn them and prepare them for persecution.

Peter himself would eventually die in that period – crucified in Rome at the hands of Nero. Jesus had predicted that he would die in this way, though when he came to be executed he requested that the cross be turned upside down, because he didn't feel worthy to be the same way up as Jesus.

Although there is no direct mention of it in Scripture, Peter had probably been ministering in that area. Paul had ministered in southern Turkey, but Peter seems to have gone to northern Turkey, and so it is to this area that he sends his letter.

The writer

We know a lot about Peter, and his first letter is a favourite among Christians. It is a warm, human letter that touches the heart. In the first chapter he tells his readers that even though they hadn't seen Jesus, they loved him and had an unspeakable joy in doing so. This love for his Saviour continues throughout the letter.

His first name was Simon or Simeon or Simone. It was a common name, though not especially complimentary – it meant 'reed'. But when Jesus met Simon, he gave him the name 'Peter', a less common name meaning 'rock', indicative of the change of character that Jesus expected. He started as a man easily swayed, like a reed in the wind, but when Jesus left him he was solid rock.

Peter was a fisherman from Bethsaida in Galilee, the brother of Andrew. They were the first two whom Jesus called to follow him. Peter is the first in every list of the Twelve and was the unofficial spokesman for the group.

Peter's character comes across very clearly in the Gospels. He has considerable strengths: he is charming, eager, impulsive and energetic. But these strengths are balanced by weaknesses: he could be unstable, fickle, weak, cowardly, rash and inconsistent. He was an impulsive man with foot-and-mouth disease – opening his mouth and putting his foot in it! But that also meant that he sometimes said wonderful things about Jesus. Many believers identify with Peter, because he is so like them.

Perhaps the most moving moment in his life came after he denied Jesus three times before Jesus' crucifixion, and then met him on the shores of Galilee after the resurrection. Jesus cooked breakfast for the disciples and Peter suddenly found himself looking into a charcoal fire. There are only two charcoal fires mentioned in the whole New Testament – the first was in the courtyard of the High Priest, when Peter was warming his hands over the fire, and denied that he knew Jesus three times. Now he is looking at a charcoal fire again, and no doubt the memory of his cowardice was still strong.

Jesus didn't say to Peter, 'I rather hoped you would be the first pastor, but I'm afraid now you will just have to give out the hymn-books.' Nor did he say, 'I am going to put you on probation for a year and see if you have pulled your socks up, and after a year we will review your case and reconsider your position.'

He actually said: 'Peter, I can cope with you, provided I am sure of one thing. Do you love me?'

This is the most important thing for any believer. Do you love him? Jesus asked Peter this same question three times, and somehow that put Peter back on track. A short time later it was Peter who was preaching at Pentecost when 3,000 were baptized. It is not surprising that the importance of love for Jesus is included in this epistle.

Peter is, of course, mentioned elsewhere in the New Testament, and was strongly involved with John Mark in the compilation of Mark's Gospel. Mark was not one of the Twelve and gleaned all his information from Peter – which is why, of all the Gospels, Mark includes Peter's weaknesses, and why Peter's own impulsive personality shines through the Gospel. In Mark, Jesus is seen as the 'man of action', not unlike Peter.

The first half of the Book of Acts is all about Peter, although because Luke wrote the book as a lawyer's brief at the trial of Paul, Peter disappears once Paul arrives on the scene.

He receives a brief, though less complimentary mention in Galatians, when Paul reflects on his heated exchange concerning Peter's refusal to have table fellowship with Gentiles in the presence of Jewish believers. Peter was wrong in his behaviour and Paul told him so.

We know he was married because Jesus healed his mother-in-law, and the apostle Paul mentions in passing that Peter took his wife with him on his missionary journeys. So we know more about Peter than any other of the apostles, with the exception of Paul.

The letter was written while Peter was in Rome. It is clear that both Peter and Paul spent some time there (Paul was under house arrest awaiting trial and was later executed at the hands of Nero), but there is no evidence that Peter was the first bishop of Rome – this is pure speculation by those who wish to believe in apostolic succession.

The readers

We are not sure how the church in Asia Minor (north-west Turkey) began, but Acts 2 records that on the day of Pentecost at Jerusalem there were people from the provinces of Cappadocia, Bithynia and Pontus, which made up Asia Minor. Maybe some people from that area were converted by Peter's first sermon, were baptized, went back home and later asked Peter to visit them.

Peter gives his readers a Jewish title, 'the Dispersion', even though they would have included many Gentiles. Just as the Jews were dispersed all over the world, so Christians were a dispersion. The name emphasizes that they were misfits. He calls them 'aliens and strangers'. The lack of specific details indicates that the letter is meant to be a circular letter for the believers in that region.

This 'misfits' label is apt, even today. One of the problems when you become a Christian is that you become a misfit. I can't stand testimonies that go like this: 'I came to Jesus and all my troubles were over.' I don't believe them, for a start, and they are so misleading. My testimony is rather different: 'I came to Jesus at 17, and my troubles began! Some years later I got filled with the Spirit, and my troubles got much worse!'

From time to time I am asked what is the evidence of being filled with the Spirit, and I always say, 'I will tell you in one word – trouble!' The reason you get into trouble is that one of the immediate effects of being filled with the Spirit is that you have a boldness of speech. This is even more common in Acts than tongues. The Greek word is *parrhesia*, meaning that you become bold to speak out. This is not the way to win friends and influence people!

Christians are misfits and no longer belong in the world. They are actually part of a new species – no longer *homo sapiens* but *homo novos* – 'new men and women', no longer in Adam, but in Christ.

This difference between a believer and those around them becomes particularly difficult, of course, when a husband or a wife is converted before their partner. Here are two people living in two different worlds. This is why the Bible teaches that a believer must not marry an unbeliever, otherwise there will be a whole area of life that they can't share.

Therefore Christians should expect trouble. Jesus was honest in telling his followers what to expect. Paul told the southern Galatian churches in Acts that 'through much tribulation we must enter the kingdom of God.' So evangelists should be honest, promising people who come to Jesus that they are in for trouble. But they can cheer up, because Jesus is on top of it.

Major themes

Turning to look at the major themes covered in 1 Peter, the first surprise is that Peter doesn't tell the believers how to escape persecution, but rather, how to endure it. The focus is on conducting themselves in a godly fashion in a hostile world, not on avoiding trouble. So suffering is at the heart of the letter and is one of the most frequently used words in it.

But Peter has two other themes. He wants to remind his readers of the salvation which is the foundation of their attitude to suffering, and then he wants to explain how to deal with suffering. Memory is a vital part of Christian living. Peter is urging them to think back to the central truths of their faith. So God's grace is a key element at the start and the end of the letter.

1. SALVATION – THROUGH CHRIST

Peter says there are two aspects of our salvation that we must be sure of – the individual and the corporate. Both are a part of being saved, though the former is more often discussed. We are saved as individuals, but we are being saved into a family which will stand us in good stead, especially when the pressure is on. We won't be able to cope by ourselves. We need to be part of a fellowship that is going to stay together.

(a) Individual – the word of God

The first focus is upon our vertical relationship with God. The individual side comes through the word of God, for it is through the word that we are born again. Peter lists the three things that follow – faith, hope and love – a triad better known at the end of 1 Corinthians 13, but which occurs all the way through Scripture. Faith is primarily relating us to what God has done in the past. Hope relates us to what he is going to do in the future, and love relates us to what he is doing in the present. Let's look at these three in more detail:

(i)   A living hope. Peter says hope is crucial as an anchor, because when the storm of persecution comes, hope will hold the believers firm. These days hope is the most neglected of the three. But the future hope is a key theme of the New Testament, and so it should be for us today.

It was certainly key for Peter's readers, for if you know that Jesus is coming back for you, it is easier to face trouble. Peter's first letter is the epistle of hope. He tells them that 'God has given us a living hope by the resurrection from the dead.' Even if you are killed, death won't touch you! We have a living hope for the future, and the hope of a new body and a new planet earth on which to live. Hope is not wishful thinking. We know we will receive our inheritance.

The real difference between a Christian who has got hope for the future and one who hasn't is this: a Christian who doesn't have hope is willing to depart and be with Christ but wanting to stay here, but a Christian with real hope wants to go but is willing to stay. Paul said, 'I am wanting to depart, but if God wants me to stay around here a little big longer, I am willing to stay.' That's the attitude we should have.

(ii) A tested faith. Peter knew the readers would very soon be undergoing the severest test. He said that our faith would be tested just as gold is refined in a fire. The fires test it, and it comes out purer. In the days when gold was purified by hand, they used a big vat. The refiner would keep stirring it over the fire until he could see his own face in it perfectly, and then he stopped refining it. This is what Peter has in mind as a picture of what God is doing with us! Our faith is tested so that we become increasingly Christlike.

(iii) A joyful love. Salvation includes a new devotion to God and to people. Peter mentions the joy in the believers' hearts in knowing that Christ is risen and alive – a joy he had experienced himself on that first Easter Sunday.

Peter is clear that salvation is both past, having been accomplished in Christ (1:10; 4:10; 5:5), and future (1:13; 3:7; 5:10). We still await the final salvation that God will bring.

(b) Corporate – the people of God

In addition to the concern for an understanding of individual salvation, Peter wants the readers to grasp the corporate dimension. Through the word of God we find individual salvation for ourselves, but that also introduces us to the people of God, an important theme for Peter.

He uses Jewish titles to describe God's people:

(i)   A spiritual house. He tells them they are a living temple, with Christ as the cornerstone and themselves as living stones. They are God's dwelling-place on earth – his holy temple. When people touch them, they are touching God's holy temple. Whenever the phrase 'you are God's temple' occurs in Scripture, 'you' is always plural, and 1 Peter is no exception. He urges the believers not to feel a sense of inferiority because of the trial they will face, but to remember who they are and whose they are.

(ii) A royal priesthood. He also describes the believers as a royal priesthood. I remember giving a lecture on the priesthood of all believers at a seminar in Zurich in Switzerland. A man came to me afterwards and said, 'That was wonderful!' – he had never heard such a thing before. But when I asked him whether he was a priest, he immediately denied it – 'No, I'm a layman'! Only after repeated questioning about whether he was a priest did he realize that according to the New Testament, the answer was yes!

Peter encourages his readers to bear their priesthood in mind when facing persecution. They must see themselves as priests, who can go to God on behalf of the people who are persecuting them. They may be the only priest their enemies will ever have.

(iii) A holy nation. Peter also urges the believers to 'be holy'. It is almost as if he has lifted the command straight out of the Book of Leviticus. Just as Israel was to be a model and example for the world of what it is like to live for God, so these believers were to do the same in the face of the persecution that would come to them. Understanding their exalted position would be a help as they sought to respond in a godly manner to the difficulties of life.

So Peter sees this discussion of salvation as a foundation. They must be absolutely sure they have the individual side of it – the faith, the hope and the love – and the corporate side, that they belong to the people of God.

2. SUFFERING

According to Peter, suffering is the inevitable result of salvation. Indeed, it is astonishing how much of the New Testament was written to Christians who were suffering, or about to suffer, persecution. Like Peter's letters, Hebrews and Revelation are written against this backdrop. Both Jesus and Paul were concerned to warn believers that they would face persecution. Western Christianity, where persecution is minimal, is actually abnormal. Peter says three things about the suffering:

(a) Make sure you don't deserve it

If you go to prison for a crime, then you certainly can't say that you are suffering for Jesus. Often we offend people with our manner or our awkwardness, and we pretend that their negative reaction is the offence of the gospel, when it is nothing of the kind. We must make sure that the only offence is the offence of the gospel. So Peter is concerned that his readers should not be deserving of any punishment they receive.

(b) Don't take revenge

When the readers suffer, Peter says they must not retaliate. The natural instinct is, of course, to hit back. Someone once told me that he didn't mind turning the other cheek when he read the Sermon on the Mount, providing he could also bring the right knee up sharply! We smile because we know how he feels.

When somebody harms us, we instinctively want to take revenge. Peter says that Christians must never do that. When Jesus suffered he did not retaliate, even when they spat on him. When a lamb was slain in the Old Testament, it was not tortured beforehand – its throat was cut quickly with a minimum of pain. But when the Lamb of God was slain, they mocked him, flogged him, jammed thorns into his forehead, dressed him up and spat on him. Yet his response was to ask his Father to forgive his enemies because they didn't realize what they were doing.

Peter says that in the same way, we should never think of getting our own back. We should repay evil with good. As Jesus said, we should 'bless those who curse us' rather than seeking to get even.

(c) Don't let it get to you

The persecutors were trying to wear down the believers, so Peter's advice was not to allow them to. He reminds the readers that although their bodies may be harmed, the persecutors are unable to touch their spirits. 'Let them do what they like with your body, but keep your spirit intact – that way, even though you seem to be losing, you will, in the end, gain the victory.'

Suffering is only for a little while, after all – a lifetime is nothing compared to eternity. Furthermore, the devil is behind all persecution, so don't see it in purely human terms.

3. SUBMISSION

As hinted earlier, Peter urges his readers to learn to submit to suffering rather than seek to avoid it. He applies this unusual advice in a number of areas. It is not blind submission, as we shall see, but it is learning to have a submissive spirit.

One of the things that astonished the world when the Jews were being carted off to extermination camps was how quietly they walked into the cremation chambers. It was an astonishing fact, because they knew what was going to happen to them. Peter is saying that the Christian must have a similar attitude.

Such behaviour is against all human instinct, the very opposite of how we normally respond to injustice. When something is unfair we generally say so. One of the earliest things children learn to say is 'It's not fair!' You hear the same sentiments expressed on picket lines outside a factory on strike.

Yet Peter is saying that Christians have no rights. They need to prepare for suffering by learning to give in and accept it. Peter perfectly exemplified this attitude when he came to be crucified himself. He didn't fight it, but insisted on being crucified upside down.

Peter covers four areas where submission is especially appropriate:

(a) Civic authorities
First, the readers should learn to submit to the civic authorities (a theme also developed in Paul's writings). They should be honest citizens, they should honour the Emperor, and they should pray for their rulers. Christians should be known as people who are glad to pay their taxes. They should not grumble about the government, but should be known as loyal subjects.

This does not mean, of course, that they are to do everything they are told. There is a limit on obedience to civic authorities. When the authorities told the apostles to stop preaching Jesus in the streets, it was Peter himself who said, 'We must obey God rather than men.' The limit comes when the authorities tell us to do something that is against the law of God. But providing this is not the case, Christians must be loyal subjects and should not be arrested because they are rebellious or aggressive towards the authorities.

(b) Slaves

It is no surprise that Christian slaves of unbelieving masters also faced suffering. The slave was the total property of his master. He had no money, time or rights of his own. Many of the masters treated their slaves abominably, and when the slaves became Christians, the masters treated them worse because they thought the slaves were getting above themselves and needed to be kept down. But in the face of this provocation, Peter urges the slaves to submit to their masters, to learn to give in and not be aggressive or resentful towards them.

(c) Christian wives

Another group that faced great suffering were Christian wives of unconverted husbands. This is a very difficult situation which causes great heartache. Peter tells wives to be subject to their husbands, which includes even the unbelieving ones. Peter gives advice on how wives can win their unconverted husband for Christ, which is totally contrary to what tends to happen. When a wife is converted before a husband, she thinks the two things she must do are preach at him and pray for him (preferably praying with all the other converted wives of all the unconverted husbands!).

Peter says neither – in fact he says that if you preach, it is the worst thing you can do. He says you have got to win him without a word. So he would have no time for the Christian wife who goes home after church and tells her husband how the sermon was ideal for him! Sadly, when the wife is converted, too many non-believing husbands say, 'Jesus ran off with my wife! She doesn't belong to me any more.'

It is very important that wives learn to go along with their husbands, but far too many women go to coffee mornings and Bible studies and become spiritual racehorses, while their husbands are still at the starting-post and feel less and less like the head of the house.

Most Christian wives later regret having preached to their husbands. By contrast, Peter says, 'Become more attractive to look at and more attractive to live with.' That is a simple programme for Christian wives. In chapter 3 Peter explains how the wife should become beautiful, though it's worth noting that he does not explain how to be glamorous. The beauty is to be inward first; the outward will follow.

(d) Young people

There is a fourth area of submission, though Peter separates it from the other three because it is not to do with suffering. He says that younger people should submit to older people, give way to them and look to them for leadership. One of the punishments the prophet Isaiah had to announce to Israel was that their failure to go God's way meant they would be ruled by women and exploited by youth – which is not irrelevant to the situation in the church today.

In all this Peter is not saying that they should blindly submit. But what Peter is saying is that whether they are young wives, or employees, they should develop the attitude of not being aggressive, of not asserting themselves or insisting on their rights.

If the devil is ultimately behind all suffering, then God needs to be behind all submission. It takes a Christlike spirit to endure suffering silently and submit to those over you. Yet in so doing, believers follow the way of their Master, who didn't retaliate when sent to the cross, but was able to say, 'Father, forgive them – they don't know what they are doing.'

A problem passage

Although 1 Peter is generally straightforward, there is one problem – a very obscure passage in chapter 3 which has at least 314 different interpretations! The passage says that Jesus was put to death in the body and made alive in the spirit, in which he went and preached to those who were disobedient in the days of Noah's flood. A few verses later Peter says, 'This is why the gospel was preached even to those who were dead, that they might be saved in their spirit.'

Liberal preachers have based their doctrine of a second chance for salvation after death on this passage, despite the fact that every other scripture says it is impossible. Death seals our fate. There is a great gulf fixed beyond death. But here, apparently, Jesus did preach to those who had died.

How should we understand it? I find that the trouble with the many interpretations is that people try to get round the simple, plain meaning of it, because it is an awkward passage to fit in with the general teaching of Scripture that death is the end of your opportunity of salvation.

I always start by taking Scripture in its simplest, plainest sense, and only change it if it really is difficult. It clearly says that between his death and resurrection Jesus was active, conscious and actually communicating with others, who were also fully conscious and communicating with him.

Now, of course, you never hear about this in church because all Holy Week services finish on Friday and start up again on Sunday, so you are never told what Jesus was doing on the Saturday! It also raises, incidentally, interesting questions about the precise events of that week. The Gospels talk of Jesus being in the tomb three days and three nights, but traditional Friday-to-Sunday interpretations leave us with one day and two nights! In fact, I believe that Jesus died on the Wednesday afternoon – all the evidence points to that. We have assumed that Friday was the day he died, because the text tells us he died on the day before the Sabbath. But in the year in question, it was not the Saturday Sabbath. John's Gospel tells us that the Sabbath was a special High Sabbath. The Passover began with a Sabbath and, in the year AD 29, which was almost certainly the year Jesus died, the first day of the Passover was a Thursday, with the Wednesday being the eve of the Passover. This fits all the evidence better than all the other theories. So if he died at 3 o'clock on the Wednesday and he rose between 6 p.m. and midnight on the Saturday, every bit of the Gospel evidence fits.

To return to Peter's passage, we tend to think of Jesus doing nothing between his death and resurrection, being just unconscious, inactive in the tomb. But it says only his body was dead. His spirit was very much alive. He went to the world of the dead and he was preaching. I can imagine Peter meeting Jesus on the first Easter Sunday and saying, 'Jesus, where on earth have you been?'

Jesus replies, 'I haven't been on earth, I have been in Hades, the world of the departed.'

'What on earth (or what in Hades!) have you been doing for three days and three nights?'

So Jesus tells Peter that he was preaching to those who were drowned in Noah's flood. This means, of course, that those who were drowned in Noah's flood were also conscious and that we will be fully conscious one minute after we have died. We will know who we are, we will have our memory. It is only our body that dies, not our spirit. Death separates body and spirit. Later, spirit and body will be reunited in the resurrection.

But Jesus went through all three phases in less than a week. He was an embodied spirit until he died on the cross. Then he commended his spirit to God, and his body was put in the tomb. Alive in the spirit, he went and preached to those disobedient people from Noah's flood. And then his body and spirit were reunited on Easter Sunday morning. But he was fully conscious and able to communicate all the way through.

If we take that at face value, it does mean that Jesus went and preached the gospel to that particular generation, and *only* to them. It does clearly imply that it was a gospel that could save them and redeem them, so isn't this a second chance after death?

I believe it was a second chance for them and for them only. There is no hint in the Bible that anyone else would ever have such an opportunity. But it seems that this was one generation who could accuse God of being unjust and unfair. They could say, 'You wiped us out and then promised never to do it again.' I believe that God wanted to make it clear that his justice and his righteousness were pure, and so he said, 'Son, go and tell them the gospel. I won't have anyone on the Day of Judgement accusing me of treating anyone unfairly.' God is righteous, and bends over backwards not to be unfair or have favourites. So maybe that is why this unusual and extreme incident arose.

So rather than to try to twist Scripture to fit our system, it is better to accept it at its simplest, plainest level. But there is no ground here for a second chance for anyone else – that is universalism, and that is not taught in Scripture.

Conclusion

Although the United Kingdom is generally free of persecution, I can anticipate increasing pressure, not least over such things as the Sex Discrimination Act, where churches will face pressure to liberalize their stance on homosexuality in the church and female elders. I can forsee the day when it will be considered an offence either to criticize another religion or even to say that your religion is better than any other. 1 Peter may one day be especially relevant to us.

The first words of Jesus that Peter heard were 'Follow me.' It is this following of Jesus that shines through in the letter. We must stand up to suffering as Jesus did. Christ was the Cornerstone, Christians are described as living stones. Christ is the Chief Shepherd, Christian leaders are under-shepherds. Just as he was hated and experienced suffering, so too will Christians. They must live as he lived.

2 Peter

This letter was written in AD 67, three years after Peter's first letter, just before he was crucified in Rome. In John's Gospel Jesus had predicted that Peter would die violently when he was old. So for 40 years he lived with the knowledge that he would be killed, though he did not know when. He says in the letter that he believes the time will be soon.

It is so different in style to 1 Peter that some scholars say it could not have been written by Peter. Its Greek is more laboured, almost as if someone was translating from one language to another using a dictionary, but with little knowledge of the grammar. Also, there are no greetings at the end or addressees at the beginning.

Indeed, 2 Peter was one of the books that were not readily accepted into the canon of the New Testament by the early church. This was partly because there were many forged documents which purported to be written by the apostles but which were in fact nothing of the sort, and partly because of the difference in style.

But the similarities are all there. Peter's favourite words still appear in the second letter as well as the first. If you go through the two letters you will find he keeps talking about our 'precious' faith and our 'precious' Jesus. Everything is 'precious' to Peter. He uses the word five times in his first letter and twice in the second.

Furthermore, he refers to his former letter (see 2 Peter 3:1). He writes of himself as an eye-witness of the Transfiguration. He knew the apostle Paul personally and spoke with him as an equal. There are words that occur in 2 Peter that are only found in 1 and 2 Peter and in Peter's speeches in Acts. So there is good reason to believe that the author of 2 Peter is indeed Peter.

So how do we account for the difference in style between Peter's two letters? I believe that Peter wrote 2 Peter, but without using Silas as a secretary, as he did with the first letter. He knows he needs to write urgently, but he doesn't know Greek well, so the grammar is more clumsy, though the meaning is clear. This would account for the difference of style quite comfortably. In some ways 2 Peter is Peter's last will and testament, just as 2 Timothy was Paul's.

Content

The letter deals with a totally different situation from his first. The readers are the same, but it's a few years later, and he feels the urgent need to address dangers inside the church. There are two kinds of pressures that churches face: the pressures from outside the church and the pressures from inside, and it is the latter that are the more dangerous. Satan has never destroyed the church from outside. The more he hits it from the outside, the bigger and stronger it gets. This is why, during the first three centuries of Christianity, when Christians were being thrown to the lions, the church grew very rapidly. This is also why today you can go to China – a nation where Christians were persecuted – and find villages where most of the population are born again. So whereas hostility was the problem in the first letter, it's heresy that is being faced in the second.

CONTRASTS BETWEEN 1 AND 2 PETER

1 Peter (AD 64)	2 Peter (AD 67)
'suffering' 16 times	'knowledge' 16 times
Danger	
Simple External Persecution	Subtle Internal Heresy
Weakness	
Compromise Anxiety	Corruption Apostasy
Status	
Birth Milk	Growth Maturity
Tone	
Comfort Wooing	Caution Warning
Hope of Christ's return	
To save The godly	To judge The ungodly

AN OUTLINE OF 2 PETER

Chapter 1: maturity to be attained
Chapter 2: morality to be maintained
Chapter 3: morale to be sustained

Peter's second letter follows exactly the same pattern as his first, which is a further proof to me that it is from the same author. There is a section on salvation, then a section on the danger. He then draws out the implications and prepares them to cope with the persecution that he knew would come.

Chapter 1: maturity to be attained

The first letter talks about new birth and the need to desire 'the milk of the word'. But in the second letter he addresses them as adults, urging them to growth and maturity. Immature Christians crave novelty; mature believers desire knowledge. He wants them to be among the second category, believing that knowledge leads to maturity.

He uses the word 'knowledge' 16 times, but never in an academic sense. He is concerned that they might have an experiential knowledge of God, based on the Scriptures. He is keen, too, that they should bring to mind all that they know about God and their faith. He uses words such as 'forgotten', 'remind', 'refresh your memory' and 'remember'. The Christian life requires constant recall of truth. This is seen supremely, of course, in eating bread and drinking wine at Communion – an ordinance designed so that we might remember Christ.

Peter's description of the mature life that every believer should seek can be summarized with a diagram showing the household of faith:

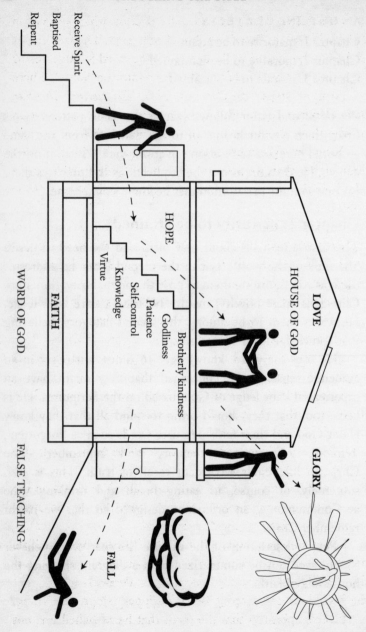

Note the steps of faith up to the front door, which are not in 2 Peter but are in Peter's sermon in Acts 2:38. The first step is 'Repent'; the second is 'Be baptized'; the third is 'Receive the Holy Spirit'. These are all steps of faith into the 'house'. There are no more steps than that. My book, *The Normal Christian Birth* (Hodder & Stoughton, 1989), gives further explanation of why these should be part of every believer's entrance into the Kingdom. We must make sure we don't raise the front door higher than we need to. Too many Bible teachers make additions that are not necessary for someone to be part of the household.

But having taken the first three steps into the household, there is a staircase. Peter says that we should add to our faith a number of qualities: virtue, knowledge, self-control, patience, godliness, brotherly kindness, and love.

In climbing the staircase of these qualities, we are building up our hope, for they help to make our calling and election sure. Indeed, this assurance can't be gained any other way. Our certainty about what God is going to do will get stronger and stronger as we progress.

So the church is founded on faith, grows in hope and is filled with love. The triad of the first letter and other parts of the Bible reappears.

There is a balcony upstairs and from that balcony you take off for glory, and you make a grand entrance into heaven. So Peter is urging his readers to progress. Don't sit down on the sofa on the ground floor. Climb the stairs, live in the upper room, get up there as quickly as you can.

So the answer to heresy is maturity. People who make little progress are vulnerable to false teaching on the ground floor. If they listen to false teaching they will find themselves going out the back door and slipping down a slippery slope and falling.

Peter emphasizes that the truth that he preached was not

his own idea. Rather, he and the other apostles and prophets had received it from God. Indeed, the prophets were often unaware of the full implications of what they were saying, serving generations to come rather than their immediate audience.

Chapter 2: morality to be maintained

This chapter in 2 Peter is almost word for word the same as the Letter of Jude. It is not, of course, the only place in the Bible where this is the case. Isaiah 2 and Micah 4 also include identical text, but questions have inevitably been raised as to how this can be.

When you come across this phenomenon in Scripture, there are five possibilities. Here they are:

1 Peter borrowed it from Jude.
2 Jude borrowed it from Peter.
3 Peter and Jude borrowed it from somewhere else.
4 Peter and Jude got together and discussed the problem and agreed on the solution, and sent it in different letters.
5 The Holy Spirit gave both of them exactly the same words.

All are possible, though I am inclined to rule out the fifth option, because the Holy Spirit doesn't use people as word processors. Our doctrine of the inspiration of Scripture must not suggest that the writers were just human typewriters. This is not how the Bible tells us that it was written. Indeed, it is unlikely that the Holy Spirit would give exactly the same words to two different people.

I prefer to say that there was collaboration. Peter was one of the inner circle of disciples and Jude was one of the Lord's own brothers, so it is highly likely that they knew each other.

In any case, the overlap material is relatively small. Jude is very short – it is the same length as 2 Peter chapter 2. The material that overlaps with Jude concerns the four corruptions that were in the church.

1. A CORRUPT CREED

Just as there were false prophets in Israel, so there were false prophets in the church. We are not told their precise message, but it is clear from the way Peter deals with the problem that two beliefs in particular were being changed. They had moved to a syncretistic view of the person of Christ and a sentimental view of the grace of God.

(a) A syncretistic view of the person of Christ

Some of the church were saying that Jesus was not the only Lord, but just one among others. He was a way to God, but there were many others. It was the word 'only' which caused offence. They were thus corrupting the person of Christ, making a Jesus of their own imagination rather than the one of the Gospels. It was not an uncommon teaching in the early church. For example, the church at Colosse was affected by such Gnostic teaching, with devastating effects.

(b) A sentimental view of the grace of God

Some professing believers thought it didn't really matter how they lived, as long as they had their ticket to heaven. Their attitude was that God loves to forgive, and will go on forgiving, no matter what you do. This is sheer sentiment and is a view preached widely today. But, of course, it means that Christians go on sinning, and take advantage of God's mercy. Such a view perverts the grace of God and leads inevitably to immorality, for there is no perception that God is concerned about how Christians live.

2. CORRUPT CONDUCT

What you believe affects your behaviour. So if individuals change or adjust the Christian faith, they will inevitably introduce error into the church. Peter describes the sins of speech that characterize their lives. He says they are bold and arrogant, slanderers, blasphemers, mouthing empty and boastful words.

Not only was their speech corrupt, but so was their behaviour. They weren't coming under the lordship of Christ. They were ignoring the commandments.

Both Peter and Jude were writing to help churches that had fallen into error. So, alas, there are some people who come into the household of faith in the correct way, but they leave by the back door. Then there are those who climb the stairs, get stronger in hope, reach the room of love and take off for glory. The former go back under the wrath and judgement of God. The latter enjoy the sunshine of his grace and favour.

3. CORRUPT CHARACTER

Corrupt character flows from corrupt conduct. There is a description of the effects of this wrong teaching on the character of people. It says that they become more animal than human, operating by base instincts rather than the Spirit of God. They become greedy and lustful and no longer reliable, for they are more driven by mood than by principle. They are like 'clouds driven by the wind', like 'waves of the sea' – vivid depictions of weak character.

4. CORRUPT CONVERSATION

Inevitably, corrupt conduct and character is seen in the kind of conversation that goes on within the church. Grumblers and complainers rebelled against the leadership, and there was the kind of unrest that leads to disunity. People not previously affected become engulfed in the gathering fire of discontent, in a manner that denies the uniting power of the gospel.

Both Peter and Jude write about this train of corruptions in order to fight them, for they knew they would finish off the church. Persecution wouldn't finish the church, because it would collapse from within. And so when persecution did come, it would be unable to stand.

Peter was thus concerned about the state of the believers within the churches. He issues some severe warnings about apostasy. He says it would be better for believers never to have known the way of righteousness than to know it, only to fall back into sin. He uses crude language to describe someone who falls away – they are like a dog going back to lick its own vomit. They came from sin and are now going back to it. Or they are like a pig that is going back to wallow in the mud after having been bathed and washed.

God is as concerned about sin in believers as he is about sin in those who are outside the church. Indeed, the person who falls away will be punished more severely than the one who never repented. It is a stark and solemn warning for those who believe they are 'safe' because they have trusted in Christ, even though their life gives a lie to their profession of faith.

Chapter 3: morale to be sustained

The final chapter in 2 Peter looks at hope for the future. Again the teaching is motivated by the concerns of the churches. Some were claiming that talk about the second coming was empty. Christ had not returned. Where was he?

So Peter replies to the scoffers. He reminds them that time is different to God. To him one day is as a thousand years. Every day that the coming is delayed is an example of God's patience. The delay is 'their salvation'. He says that one day all the universe will be dissolved in fire. There is to be another holocaust, and this time it will be not a flood of water, but a flood of fire. I don't imagine that it will be a nuclear war; I think God will release all the energy in every atom. He packed the energy into the atom, so all he would need to do would be to unlock it, and the whole world would go up in smoke.

But Peter concludes the section by reminding his readers that out of the fire, like a phoenix rising from the flames, there will be a new heaven and a new earth. I love preaching about the new earth. Don't leave it to the Jehovah's Witnesses – it is a Christian truth, it is in the Bible! But I am afraid Christians only want to hear about going to heaven – which is, after all, just a waiting-room we go to before we enter into all that God has for us.

The theme of the new earth coming is developed by John at the end of Revelation. This earth is going to be the centre of the future. Christians are the only ones who know this. Everybody is panicking about the ozone layer and the polluted oceans and the dying forests. They are concerned because they think this is the only planet we will ever have to live on. We know better than that; we look for a new heaven and a new earth. We know there is going to be something that will be different from this planet we have known, for it will be a new heaven and earth in which righteousness will dwell. There will be no vice, no crime, no sin, nothing dirty, nothing filthy.

Peter says that if we keep our hope fixed on this, we will live the way that we will be living in that new world. We won't listen to the false teaching and won't get caught up in it and tainted by it. We will keep ourselves unspotted from the apostate church, never mind the world.

So a godly hope is his real defence against the immorality that can get into the church through false teaching. Keep your eyes fixed on that new world, a world of righteousness which will keep you living right, because you know that if you don't, you won't be part of that new world. It is as we live in faith, hope and love that we get ready for glory. When you hear the sound of the trumpet, you will have your first free flight to the Holy Land!

On my grandfather's tombstone in Newcastle there are three words from an old Methodist hymn. There is his name, 'David Ledger Pawson', and underneath, 'What a Meeting'. If you don't like noisy worship, don't be around then, for the archangel will be shouting and trumpets will be blowing. It will be enough to raise the dead, which is exactly what it will do. Those who have died will get front seats, so don't worry if you die first.

Peter finishes with a stark choice. We can either ignore his teaching and be among those who fall away, or we can be those who continue to grow in the grace of Christ. Peter said God was able to keep Lot even in Sodom and Gomorrah. And so he can keep you too.

PART IV

JUDE

Introduction

A neglected book

Jude has been called 'the most neglected book in the New Testament'. There are a number of reasons for this:

1. IT'S SMALL

Along with Philemon and 2 and 3 John, it is one of the smallest books in the New Testament.

2. IT'S STRANGE

Readers are puzzled by the reference to the Archangel Michael arguing with Satan over Moses' body. What does that refer to? The references to 'the sons of Korah' and to angels locked in a dungeon seem similarly obscure. What did the sons do and why are angels locked up in a dungeon?

3. IT'S SUSPECT

Some people take exception to the way Jude quotes the Apocrypha. The Apocrypha is the name given to the Jewish books written in the 400 years between the end of Malachi and the beginning of Matthew – books included in the Catholic version of the Bible but not in the Protestant Bible. These writings never claim to be the word of God, for they do not include the phrase, 'Thus says the Lord', which occurs 3,808 times in the Old Testament – hence their omission from the Protestant Bible. God didn't speak during the 400 years between the Testaments. There were no prophets to speak for him. These writings are not prophetic, but this does not mean that they do not have value or do not contain true statements. So Jude's quotations from the Apocrypha need not cast doubt on Jude, just because apocryphal writings are not canonical. The writings were well known and so proved valuable to back up his point.

4. IT'S SEVERE

Jude comes across as negative and intolerant, as he seeks to warn the believers and challenge them to action.

5. IT'S SHARP

Jude is like a surgeon wielding a knife to cut out the cancer in the body of Christ. Hence some of the language is strong, as he condemns evil teaching.

PRESSURES

Jude's sharp tone is necessary on occasion, especially as internal pressures from errant teachers can create such havoc among the people of God. Churches face danger from two sources:

External

Pressure from persecution will always be possible, though at different levels. Today the church is undergoing what may be termed 'persecution' in 225 countries. But during external pressure, the church continues to thrive.

Internal

Pressure from within is the greater cause for concern. Paul's Letter to the Galatians explains how legalism and liberalism within the church gave great concern in the early years of its life. Jesus condemned both the legalism of the Pharisees and the liberalism of the Sadducees. Yet these dangers are all too evident in churches, especially in second-generation ones. They can become too narrow-minded, imposing standards of discipline that go beyond the requirements of the Bible. Or they can become too lax, failing to impose any discipline on behaviour that is contrary to apostolic practice.

The different views can be summed up like this. Legalism says you are *not free to sin*, and we are going to see that you don't. Licence says you are *free to sin* and it is OK now that you are a Christian – you have your ticket to heaven, so you needn't worry. But the true liberty of Christianity says, 'You are *free not to sin*. Sin does matter in the life of the believer, but Christ has freed you from its power.' So Jude's concerns are no different from those of Jesus and the apostle Paul. Jude is a profound epistle with a message that is vital for the church today.

But having explained some of its difficulties, there is no doubt that it is a challenging book to understand. I've paraphrased it to bring out its meaning a little more clearly.

A paraphrase

This letter comes from Judas – Jude for short – one of the slaves bought by King Jesus, and a brother of the James you know well.

It is addressed to those who have been called out of the world, who are now loved ones in the family of God, their Father, and who are being kept for presentation to King Jesus. May you have more and more of the mercy, peace and love you have already experienced.

Loved ones, I was fully intending to correspond with you about the wonderful salvation we share, but found that I had to write quite a different kind of letter. I must urge you to keep up the painful struggle for the preservation of the true faith that was passed on to the early saints once and for all. I've heard that certain persons, who shall be nameless, have sneaked in among you – godless men whose sentence of doom was pronounced long ago. They twist the free grace of God into an excuse for blatant immorality, and they deny that King Jesus is our only Master and Lord.

Now I want to remind you of some of those absolute truths which you already know perfectly well, particularly that God is not someone to be trifled with. You will recall that the Lord brought a whole nation safely out of Egypt, but the next time he intervened, they were all exterminated for not trusting him.

Nor were his angels any more exempt than his people. When some of them deserted their rank and abandoned their proper station, he took them into custody and is keeping them permanently chained in the lowest and darkest dungeon until their trial on the great Day of Judgement.

And in the same way, the inhabitants of Sodom and Gomorrah, together with those from two neighbouring towns, glutted themselves with gross debauchery, craving for unnatural intercourse, just as the angels had done. And the fate they suffered in the fire that burned for ages is a solemn warning to us all.

In spite of such examples in history, these people who have wormed their way into your fellowship pollute their own bodies in exactly the same manner. They belittle divine authority and smear angels in glory. Yet even the chief of all angels – Michael, whose very name means 'godlike' – did not dare to accuse Satan directly of blasphemy when they were arguing about who owned the body of Moses, and he was content to leave accusations to God himself and said simply, 'The Lord rebuke you.'

But these men among you don't hesitate to malign whatever they don't understand, and the only things they do understand will prove their undoing in the end, for their knowledge of life comes only from their animal instincts, like brute beasts without any capacity for reason. Woe betide them! They've gone down the same road as Cain. They have rushed headlong into the same mistake as Balaam, and for the same motivation – money. They will come to the same end as Korah did in his rebellion.

These people have the cheek to eat with you at your fellowship meals of love, though they are only looking for pasture for themselves. Like submerged rocks, they could wreck everything. They're like clouds driven past so hard by the wind that they give no rain. They are like uprooted trees in autumn, with neither leaves nor fruit, doubly dead. They are like wild waves of the sea, stirring up the filthy foam of their own odious disgrace. They are like shooting stars falling out of orbit, destined to disappear down a black hole forever.

Enoch, who lived only seven generations after the first man, Adam, saw all this coming. He was referring to these very people when he made his prophetic announcement, 'Look out! The Lord has arrived with ten thousand of his angels to put all human beings on trial and convict all godless people of all the godless deeds they have committed in their godless lives, and of the hard things they have spoken against him. These people are discontented grumblers, always complaining and finding fault. Their mouths are full of big talk about themselves, but they're not above flattering others when it is to their advantage.

Now, loved ones, you should have remembered what the apostles of our Lord Jesus Christ said would happen. They predicted that in the final age there are bound to be those who pour scorn on godliness, whose lives will only be governed by their own godless cravings. People like this can only create divisions among you, since they only have their natural instincts to go by and they lack the guidance of the Spirit.

As for you, loved ones, be sure to go on building yourselves up on the solid foundation of your most holy faith, praying in the way the Spirit gives you. Stay in love with God, waiting patiently for the time when our Lord Jesus Christ in his sheer mercy will bring you into immortal living. As regards the others, here is my advice. To those who are still wavering, be especially kind and gentle. Those who have already been led into error must be snatched from the fire before they are badly burned. And those who have been thoroughly contaminated should be treated better than they deserve, though you must never lose a healthy fear of being infected yourself, even by their stained underwear. Let's just praise the one Person who is able to keep you from stumbling and to make you stand upright in his glorious presence without any imperfection, but with great jubilation – the only God there is, and he's our Saviour too, through Jesus Christ our Lord. For to him alone belongs all glory, all majesty, all power and all authority, before history began, now in this present time, and for all ages to come. So it will be. [That's what the word 'Amen' means.]

WHO IS JUDE?

Jude was the second youngest brother of Jesus. His real name is Judas, shortened to Jude, to distinguish him from the apostle who betrayed Jesus.

When we examined the letter written by James, one of his other brothers, we noted that the brothers of Jesus didn't believe in him during his lifetime. This is made clear by their scepticism about his claims to messiahship recorded in John's Gospel (John 7:4). It was at the time of the Feast of

Tabernacles in Jerusalem, and they teased him about his claims to be sent by God. Everyone knew that if the Messiah came, it would be during the Festival, so they said he had better go and show himself. Jesus told them that the time was not right to say who he was publicly, but he did go to the Feast secretly.

But after the resurrection, the situation changed and his brothers became missionaries for Jesus. James and Jude wrote two letters and were both careful to play down their family relationship with Jesus, preferring to focus on their spiritual relationship. They both refer to themselves as 'a slave of Jesus'.

Content

Moral pollution

It is clear that Jude intended to write a quite different letter. In the early part of the letter he says, 'I wanted to write about the salvation we enjoy in Jesus.' But when he heard what was happening in the churches he was writing to, he changed his mind. So he adds, 'I'm pleading with you to keep up the painful struggle for the faith that was once delivered to the saints' (my translation).

The word 'painful' indicates the intensity of the struggle. Indeed, it is the most painful struggle that they will ever have. It is especially painful because it is their own brothers and sisters they have to deal with. The struggle concerns heretical teachers who were leading the church astray. Jude knew they would continue to pollute the membership if they were not checked.

The first half of the letter is about a very dangerous corruption that has crept into the churches to which he is writing. Then the second half tells them how to deal with that situation in a delicate way. We shall look first at the four phases whereby the corruption affects the church.

1. CREED

Jude outlines how people have secretly wormed their way into the fellowship. The implication is that their actions were underhand, and their intentions evil. They poisoned the fellowship with their teaching and their behaviour, and so must be dealt with. False teaching was like a cancer spreading throughout the body, and would result in death if it wasn't dealt with. It is clear that the false teaching was similar to that which Peter wrote against in his second letter, which is why the two letters share an identical section. I believe Jude used 2 Peter as part of his research and was happy to include part of it word for word.

There were two areas in particular in which the false teachers were errant. They had a sentimental view of God and a syncretistic view of Jesus.

(a) A sentimental view of God

Their sentimental view of God made God's grace an excuse for immorality. They saw God as a 'nice old boy' who pats you on the head and says, 'Let's forgive and forget. All I want you to be is happy.' That's the caricature of God that is too often preached on TV – a nice, comfortable God who wouldn't harm a fly. It's a sentimental view of God, but not a scriptural one. God doesn't overlook sin, he deals with it. We need to recover that non-sentimental but scriptural view of God.

(b) A syncretistic view of Jesus

They also had a syncretistic view of Jesus. They no longer believed that Jesus was the only Master and Lord, and sought to put him on a level with others – a situation all too common in the present day. Once you put Jesus in a pantheon with Mohammed and Buddha and all the rest, he is no longer the only way to God. He is no longer 'the way, the truth and the life' but 'a way, a truth and a life'.

2. CONDUCT

Once you've corrupted a church's creed, it's not long before their conduct goes haywire as well. Ultimately belief determines behaviour, so Jude comes to the severest part of his warning. He reminds the believers of what had happened to three groups in history.

(a) Israel in the wilderness

Jude recalls the story from Exodus 32 of the children of Israel in the wilderness, who made a golden calf and quickly fell into immorality and idolatry. Their view of God departed from the one given by Moses in the Ten Commandments and subsequent teaching. As a consequence, they developed a wrong view of each other and started mistreating each other, rather than loving each other in the way they had been taught. The result was that none of them got into Canaan. They had been redeemed from Egypt but they didn't get into the Promised Land. They started out but none of them finished.

This incident is used three times in the New Testament by three different writers to warn Christians that it's not those who start but those who finish who will inherit all that God has for them. Paul uses it, the writer to the Hebrews uses it, and here Jude uses it.

So the warning is clear: if the children of Israel were redeemed from Egypt but didn't make it to the Promised Land, that can also happen to the believer today. It's not just what you've left behind, it's what's still ahead. It's not yours yet – you need to persevere if you are not to perish in the wilderness.

(b) The angels at Mount Hermon

Jude looks at what happened to the angels at Mount Hermon. We know details of this from the Book of Enoch in the Apocrypha (though, as we have noted, the Apocrypha is not part of the Bible).

In the region of Mount Hermon about 200 angels seduced women and impregnated them. This horrible intercourse between angels and humans spawned ghastly hybrid creatures called the Nephilim – thankfully, they have all died out. We can't be sure what they were like – they are known as 'giants' in some translations. God has his order of life, and angels having sex with human beings is as offensive to him as human beings having sex with animals.

The result of this behaviour was that violence filled the earth, and perverted sex and occultism were rampant. We even read in Genesis that God was grieved that he had ever made humankind – in my view, that is one of the saddest verses in the Bible.

So Jude is saying that if God's people Israel didn't escape judgement and the angels didn't escape judgement, how do you think you will as Christians?

(c) Sodom and Gomorrah

The third example concerns Sodom and Gomorrah. These cities are well known, but there were also Admah and Zeboiim, making four cities at the southern end of the Dead Sea. In due course they have all been engulfed by an earthquake. The Dead Sea is like a figure-of-eight. The cities are under the most southerly part which is now drying up. So Sodom and Gomorrah could reappear in our lifetime. What a symbolic event that would be!

We know from the Jewish historian Josephus that the fire that destroyed Sodom and Gomorrah 2,000 years before Jesus was still burning in Jesus' day. When Jesus spoke of it in his talks, the hearers could just walk for 30 minutes outside Jerusalem and see the smoke.

These two cities were punished because they went against God's laws. Homosexual relationships became tolerated, just as today the criticism of same-sex unions is regarded as politically incorrect and a form of sex discrimination.

Jude is warning the Christians that God will judge them if they follow the same pattern. God is not to be trifled with. He loathes idolatry (which hurts him) and immorality (which hurts those he has made). He may not deal with them immediately, but ultimately all moral pollution of his creation must be punished.

3. CHARACTER

When your creed is corrupted, your conduct will soon follow. When your conduct is corrupted, your character will go the same way. Character is the result of conduct – an act reaps a habit, a habit reaps a character, a character reaps a destiny. So the third phase in the moral pollution of the church is that their character becomes increasingly worldly. Jude focuses next on the characters of the false teachers and their similarity to the characters of three people in the Old Testament.

(a) Cain

He starts with Cain, who killed his brother out of jealousy (Genesis 4). He tells the readers that the false teachers are motivated in part by jealousy, just like Cain, and so are bound to affect those who listen.

(b) Balaam

He continues with Balaam the prophet, who was offered money to prophesy against Israel (Numbers 22). The love of money had so taken hold of Balaam that God had to speak to him through his donkey! Balaam was a man of avarice, as Cain was a man of anger.

(c) Korah

Korah was a man of ambition who was jealous of Moses and wanted to set up his own show (Numbers 16). He completes a rather depressing triad. There are modern parallels to Korah. New churches can be great, but it is clear that some are being set up for the wrong reasons. They are set up because a man wants his own show – a modern 'son of Korah' who doesn't accept God-given leadership and wants his own way. In the end Korah was swallowed up in judgement with 250 others who perished because of their defiance of the authority that God had invested in Moses.

All three of these charcters were governed by self, and all three caused death to others. They depict the kind of characters that will emerge in the church if it doesn't deal with false teaching. Anger, avarice and ambition will all be prominent.

4. CONVERSATION

But these weren't the only problems they faced. Once character is corrupted, conversation will also be corrupted, because conversation flows out of character. Jude describes the sort of speaking which characterizes the people who have wormed their way into the fellowship. Sure signs of inner decay are constant grumbling and complaining, muttering and moaning, contempt for inferiors, flattery for superiors, scorn and ridicule for whatever is not understood and, above all, rejection of anyone else's authority. Beware of people who join your fellowship because they are dissatisfied with another fellowship – in six months' time they'll be dissatisfied with yours! Grumblers and fault-finders on the move are always looking for the perfect fellowship. The old saying is true:

'If you're looking for the perfect fellowship, don't join it, because you're bound to spoil it!'

A puzzling passage

Perhaps the most puzzling verses in Jude concern an angel arguing with the devil about the body of Moses. It refers back to an extraordinary statement at the end of Deuteronomy, where we are told that Moses died on Mount Nebo but 'no one knows where his grave is to this day.' So if no one was with him and nobody knows where his grave is – who buried him? The answer is that God sent the angel Michael to bury Moses. Angels are very practical people. They're good cooks (Elijah found out that angels can cook a jolly good meal) and they can ride chariots (as Elijah also discovered). In the modern day I have heard of angels in Afghanistan riding bicycles, protecting a missionary who was on his bike! Angels don't come with shiny white nightdresses, wings, harps and long blond hair. Hebrews 13 speaks of 'entertaining angels unawares', which certainly wouldn't be possible if their appearance was that strange. They look like normal humans.

So this angel was sent with a spade to bury the body of Moses, but when he got there the devil was standing over the body and told him that the body was his. It is instructive to note that in the confrontation that follows Michael didn't even rebuke Satan. We can be very cheeky with Satan and we are very foolish if we are. He's far cleverer than we are. It worries me when I hear young people say, 'We rebuke you, Satan.' Michael actually said, 'The Lord rebuke you', and the devil went and Michael buried Moses properly.

Dealing with corruption

Having looked at the four areas of Jude's concern – creed, conduct, character and conversation – we next need to ask how we should face similar difficulties today.

1. WE SHOULD EXPECT PROBLEMS

The first thing is not to be surprised when things go wrong in the church. Some Christians are over-alarmed, but both the Old Testament prophets and the New Testament apostles told us to expect things to go wrong. Jesus himself warned us about wolves in sheep's clothing. Why are we so surprised when their predictions come true? After all, we're not yet entirely saved and so there are bound to be problems in the church. It's the way we deal with them that is important. We should be unshockable, take them in our stride and deal with them.

2. WE MUST RESIST WHAT IS HAPPENING

It is intriguing to note that Jude does not indict Satan for this havoc. He places the blame firmly at the door of 'these men' who are responsible for causing trouble. And he makes it quite clear that some in the church will have the job of speaking out against error. Man must deal with it – it's not God's job. Jude mentions the ministry of Enoch, the very first prophet in the Bible – the first man to get a message from the Lord for other people. It was a warning that God was going to come in judgement and deal with that whole generation. He was 65 years old when he had a son, and he asked God what he should call him. God gave him an extraordinary name for the son. He said, 'Call him "When he dies it will happen"' – though we know him as Methuselah. It's clear that he lived longer than anybody else, because God is so patient that he waited almost a millennium before judgement came. On the day that Methuselah died, it began to rain. But by that time Methuselah's grandson

Noah had built a boat. God waited 969 years before judging that generation. It was Martin Luther who said, 'If I was God I'd have kicked the whole world to bits long ago.'

Jude was especially keen to point out that the behaviour of the false teachers was 'godless'. He uses the word five times in all. Godliness had become an object of their scorn. The New Testament apostles warned us that in the last days there will be scoffers and godliness will be a joke. There are times when Christians are a laughing-stock because they want to be godly and it goes against the grain. Godlessness is the 'in' thing, and anyone who thinks otherwise is regarded as odd.

3. WE CAN REDUCE THE EXTENT OF THE DAMAGE

Jude next gives practical advice on how the believers should protect themselves and others.

(a) Themselves

The first way to deal with it was for the believers to make sure they were right with God and to build themselves up in faith, hope and love.

The stronger we are, the more likely we are to stand firm. The best way to avoid sickness is to foster health. Jude urges the strengthening of the familiar triad of faith, hope and love. Healthy living includes praying in the Spirit, keeping God's commandments and living for the future, realizing that God intends that we should be holy, not necessarily happy. After all, compared to the 'happiness' we will enjoy in eternity, we shouldn't be concerned if life is tough. It is crucial to note that we are responsible for looking after ourselves and building ourselves up. God won't do it for us.

(b) Others

There were three categories of people who needed help.

(i) Those with mental doubts. Jude urges the believers to help those who are wavering. They are wondering whether to follow these teachers or not, and are in mental doubt. They must be talked to, even argued with, but always in a tender rather than a tough way. Harshness could drive them further into error.

(ii) Those in mortal danger. Next, there will be others who have been led further into mortal danger because they have already started to believe the new ideas. Jude says the believers should 'snatch them from the fire' – they should regard them as being in a house on fire and should get them out any way they can! The phrase 'snatch them from the fire' has been used in evangelism to mean snatching people from the fire of hell, although these verses have nothing to do with that. Yes, it's snatching people from the fire of hell, but not because they're unsaved, but because they're Christians who are going to be led astray. Even those who were spreading the falsehood must not be written off but given a chance to repent.

(iii) Those morally defiled. The third category of people concerns those who are defiled. The Greek says we should be very, very wary of being infected by them, even by their stained underwear! It seems a strange phrase to use, but it's obvious that there are diseases that are introduced through sexual perversion and promiscuity that we need to be afraid of.

4. WE CAN AVOID WHAT IS HAPPENING

Jude's message is that we should not be surprised by attacks on the faith, but should deal with them and remember all the time that God is able to keep us from falling. It's important, however, that we strike a balance when reading verses that speak of God's keeping power. There are a series of texts in the Bible which affirm God's keeping power, but they are invariably close to ones which emphasize our need to remain close to him. So the penultimate verse of Jude doesn't say, 'God is certain to keep you from falling', but says, 'he is *able* to help you to keep yourself in him.' It's not all on us and it's not all on him – it's 'Keep yourself in him, for he is able to keep you. Go on trusting him and you won't fall.'

We can say that he has the ability to keep us and present us before God, providing we remain faithful. He also has the authority, for he is the only God and only Saviour.

So Jude finishes with a note of praise. In spite of the evil teaching and the attendant dangers, God is able to keep us and present us faultless before him on the Last Day. There's no question about it. If God is on our side (the real meaning of the name Immanuel, 'God with us'), we can fight and win. So be it!

Conclusion

There's one clear message from studying the letters of the New Testament. The biggest danger to the church is from the inside. We've got to watch it all the time and in truth and love contend for the gospel that was 'once delivered' to the saints. There's a big battle on right now in the Western world to do just that. We must be clear about the truth. If you don't believe that my writing fits with what your Bible says, then forget it. But if you do find it there, then cling to it and fight for it and contend for the faith once delivered to the saints! It may not sound like glamorous work, but it's crucial if church fellowships are going to remain strong.

So although Jude is one of the most neglected books in the New Testament, its message is ever relevant and needs to be heard by the church today if it is not to be increasingly riddled with the same problems.

PART V

1, 2 AND 3 JOHN

Introduction

There are two sorts of letter in the New Testament. Some are general or circular letters with no specific recipients – rather like tracts. Others are personal, reflecting what the readers needed to hear.

John's letters are a mixture of the two. His first is general and, at five chapters, is much longer than the others, as John addresses particular concerns that he has for the believers. The second and third are more personal and are the shortest books in the New Testament. In these John addresses two separate individuals, using just one sheet of papyrus for each.

The letters are warm and personal, reflecting the character of this saint, who is now probably in his eighties. Some call them 'fatherly letters', but given his age, 'grandfatherly' might be a more appropriate description.

They were written at a time when the church was being affected for good or ill by travelling Bible teachers. John is very concerned about the damage that some are causing, but is too elderly to travel – unlike the false teachers who, it seems, are able to promote their heresy with considerable vigour. Hence these letters were his best way of addressing the problem.

John was one of the twelve apostles called by Jesus during his earthly ministry, and the only one to live to an old age. Extra-biblical records state that he looked after Mary, the mother of Jesus, in Ephesus until she died. He too died there. His letters breathe with the authority not just of an elder, but of *the* elder. For here is one who has had personal contact with Christ (see 1:2; 2:1; 4:6, 14).

Some Bible scholars argue that the apostle John did not write the letters. It is certainly a surprise that there are not more references to the Old Testament than his single reference to Cain killing Abel – especially as the Book of Revelation, also by John, has over 400 references. But when you compare the letters to John's Gospel, they have the same style and vocabulary. Expressions found in the Gospel, such as 'eternal life', 'new commandment' and 'remain in Christ', which are special to John, are also in the letters, and in some cases identical phrases are found – for example, 'walking in darkness' and 'that your joy may be full'.

Furthermore, both the Gospel and the letters describe the Christian life with absolute contrasts. John's assessment of the world is in sharp contrast to the modern vogue of relativism, which believes that distinctions are inappropriate – nothing is true or false – everything is just an opinion. John, and the rest of the Bible, stand against this view. John draws a number of contrasts: life and death, light and darkness, truth and lies, love and hate, righteousness and lawlessness, children of God and children of Satan, love of the Father and love of the world, Christ and antichrist and – the biggest contrast of all – heaven and hell. Such opposites give no room for a 'third way'. You are either one or the other, and there are no further options.

So although there is no name on the manuscripts, internal evidence points strongly to John as the author. Furthermore,

Irenaeus and Papias, two early church fathers, confirm that the letters came from John's pen.

There is no date given, but it seems likely that the letters were written after John's Gospel, and before John's exile on Patmos, where he wrote the Book of Revelation. There is no reference to Domitian's terrible attacks on the church, which came in AD 95, so a date of around AD 90 is likely.

1 John

John's readers

We have noted that the first letter is a general letter with no specific destination as such. But there are clear categories of reader that John has in mind. These come in 2:12–14, where John addresses his letter to three groups of people: 'little children', 'young men' and 'fathers'.

It is not physical ages but spiritual ages that are in view. The 'little children' are the recent converts, who need to be given milk rather than meat to help them grow. John says the little children have experienced two things: they know forgiveness, and they know God is the Father, but they know little else.

The 'young men' are those who have grown up and matured. John says three things about them: they have grown a bit stronger than weak babies, they have digested Scripture, and they have known victory in battles with Satan.

John is also writing to much older Christians whom he calls 'fathers'. Their experience has both length and depth. Here are people whose experience of God is very rich.

Modern eyes will notice that John puts the groups into a male form. This is not unusual, for the whole New Testament is addressed to 'brothers', not 'brothers and sisters'. We need to explain this male emphasis, especially in a day of 'non-sexist' or 'inclusivist' Bibles and confusion about the appropriate gender to give to God.

The main reason for the male focus of Scripture is that the strength and character of the church can be seen in its men. Men have the responsibility of leadership in the church as well as in the home, and it is their character that will determine the strength of the whole church. This is one reason why I have spent so much time setting up and speaking at 'Men for God' conferences. Most of the letters I have received have been from women delighted at the change in their husbands! Sadly, I would be a wealthy man if I had a £10 note for every family in the church where the wife is ahead of the husband spiritually. It's healthy where the husband is ahead of the wife, for the husband can't be a head unless he's ahead. But, of course, this is not to imply that women are inferior in any way, merely that the roles are complementary.

John's reasons for writing

It is clear that John's first concern in writing is pastoral. He refers to the readers as his 'little children'. He has great affection for them, but is unable to visit them all. There are hints in the text that he may have particular concerns in mind. There are two ways of examining John's reasons for writing:

LIST 1

He wants his readers to be:

> *Satisfied* (1:4). He writes 'that their joy may be full', implying that they are dissatisfied with life.
> *Sinless* (2:1). He is concerned that they should live blameless lives.
> *Safe* (2:26). He wants them to be safe from all the wiles of the devil, especially false teaching, which is the devil's

particular approach to church life and which was affecting the believers he wrote to.

Sure (5:13). Above all, he wants the readers to be sure of what they believe. Christians need to be assured. There's a doctrine of assurance in these little letters that is very important. We don't want to be waking up every morning insecure, but to be sure of who we are in Christ. We need to 'know' (a key word here) that we are in God's hands.

LIST 2

On the other hand, an alternative way of examining the motives would be as follows. He is writing:

> to promote harmony among them (1:3);
> to produce happiness (1:4):
> to protect holiness (2:1);
> to prevent heresy (2:26);
> to provide hope (5:13).

What is clear is that he is writing about 60 years after he first heard Jesus say 'Follow me.' He is an old man, and I can imagine him with a long beard saying, 'I'm your grandfather in the faith. I want you to be satisfied and sure of who you are, and I want you to be holy, and in harmony and full of hope.' So there is a very tender pastoral heart writing these letters.

An outline of 1 John

Although we can discern John's motives in writing, it is not so easy to find any pattern in the way he has arranged his material. The letter is almost impossible to analyse because he seems to go round in circles. His thinking is cyclic rather than linear. I'm a linear man – I like to see the progress of an argument and to analyse. The apostle Paul, with his legal mind, writes that way. So I find myself a little lost when I come to a man who thinks in circles and goes round the same themes. John's circular style can be explained by his profession, his age and his nationality.

1. HIS PROFESSION

John is a fisherman, not a lawyer like Paul, and so is apt to move from one subject to the next as if he's having a conversation. He wasn't an educated man and so hadn't been taught to think in linear patterns.

2. HIS AGE

Old men tend to become garrulous – they talk round and round things – it is characteristic of age. Listeners need to concentrate to pick up the wisdom they impart.

3. HIS NATIONALITY

But I think the major reason is that John follows the fashion of the Jews, who tend to talk like the book reads. Both the Book of Proverbs in the Old Testament and James in the New visit and revisit a number of subjects. Anyone seeking a systematic study on an area in these books needs to hunt all the way through. There's no real structure in them.

WORLD OR WORD?

One way of looking at 1 John is to focus upon a theme which John develops throughout the epistle, using the diagram opposite.

THE WORD

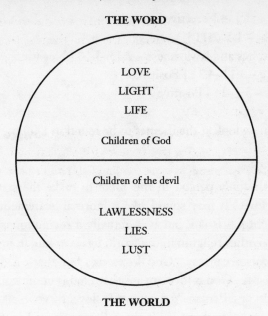

LOVE

LIGHT

LIFE

Children of God

Children of the devil

LAWLESSNESS

LIES

LUST

THE WORLD

The diagram shows a world with two hemispheres. The one half is governed by the word of God – it is a world of life, love and light. The other half is governed by the world – lawlessness, lies and lust. John is urging his readers to live by the word of God. He is telling them that he wants them to focus on the word of God and not be tempted to listen to the world. Every Christian has to make this choice. If you love the world, you will soon be living that kind of life. If you love the word, you will be living in an altogether different kind of way.

This simple framework helps us to see that there is some shape to the letter. It begins positive, then turns negative, and then turns positive again – a pleasing sandwich with twice as much positive as negative. We need both; we need to know what to believe and what not to, how to behave and how not to.

So the 'sandwich' structure of 1 John can be summarized as follows:

Life – 1:1–4 } Positive
Light – 1:5–2:11 }
Lust, lies and lawlessness – 2:15–3:10 } Negative
Love – 3:11–4:21 } Positive
Life – 5:1–21 } Positive

We will now look at the themes to be found in 1 John.

Love

John is the only person in the Bible to make the statement, 'God is love.' It may sound like a 'normal' statement to the well-taught Christian, but it is actually a revolutionary statement. No other religion in the world has ever said it, nor could they. Judaism can say, 'God loves us', but that's a different thing. To say, 'God is love' means that God is understood to be more than one Person. You cannot *be* 'love' by yourself. So it is because we know that God is three Persons – Father, Son and Holy Spirit – that we can say, 'God is love.' Before the world came into being, there were the Father, the Son and the Holy Spirit, who all loved each other.

People sometimes ask, 'Why did God make us?' At the simplest level, God had one Son, and he loved him so much that he wanted a bigger family. He wanted to share the love he already had with a larger circle – that's why he wanted to make many sons.

Heresy

As well as general concern for the readers' spiritual well-being, John is also facing specific problems, and writes to counter the false teaching that he knows is affecting them. At different points in the letter he refers to 'they' (as opposed to 'we' and 'you'), meaning a group of teachers known to the church.

The false teachers taught Greek philosophy, which included

a number of elements that contradicted the biblical worldview. Crucially, they taught that there was a necessary separation between the physical and the spiritual.

We imbibe this disintegrated outlook on life, even today. For example, you will never find the distinction between 'sacred' and 'secular' in the Bible, and yet even Christians say to me, 'I'm in a secular job.' I always reply that they are in no such thing. Unless a job is immoral or illegal, it is not secular. There is nothing secular except sin. Indeed, I made this point once in the North of England, and a nationally known pop singer was converted. He thought he was in a secular job, part of which was making the jingles for advertisements on TV. My words helped him to realize that he could do his work for the glory of God.

Those promoting Greek philosophy also believed that the physical was evil, and only the spiritual was good. So the body was evil, and the soul good. They gave people the impression that anything physical was somehow dirty or sinful. This underlying philosophy had repercussions for what the church believed and the way she behaved. Let us look at belief first.

1. BELIEF

John's biggest concern was that the false teachers applied this thinking to Jesus. They found it impossible to accept that God could be a man. They reasoned that God is eternal and man is in time. God is spiritual and man is physical. So how could God be a man on earth?

This belief took many different forms. One was the belief that Jesus didn't come in the flesh but only appeared to. It is a heresy called 'docetism', which means simply 'to put on a mask, 'to appear'. John says in this letter that if you hear someone say that Jesus hasn't come in the flesh, you know that view is inspired by the devil. John was at pains to point out that he had seen and touched Jesus himself. He was flesh and bones, and indeed still is. The so-called New Age philosophy is teaching something similar when it separates the human Jesus from the divine Christ.

Another heresy said that Jesus was a human being until his baptism at the age of 30, when 'the Christ' came upon him. Then, at his death, 'the Christ' went away again, and it was 'Jesus' who died and was buried. So in this theory, 'Jesus' and 'the Christ' are actually two different entities.

In the same way, the New Age teachers talk about Christ but don't like the name Jesus. They say that everyone can have the Christ come upon them. It is very subtle and it fools a lot of people, who believe that because the New Age is using biblical language, with biblical meaning. One of the favourite statements of New Age teachers is that God is outside time, that he is timeless – a belief not uncommon amongst Christians. Actually the Bible never says that God is timeless. It says that God is everlasting, which is quite a different thing. Time is real to God. God is the God who was and who is and who is to come. God isn't in time; rather, time is in God.

The Greeks also separated God entirely from time, and this belief is still around today. You would be amazed how many Christians think that when we go to heaven, we go outside time. We don't – we go into everlasting life. Time is extended infinitely. Time is real in God, and time is real in the Bible, and therefore history is 'his story'.

But, of course, these teachers believed they were 'in the know'. Their knowledge was superior to the church. It was a form of Gnosticism, which was to dog the church for centuries, and is still around in different guises today.

So John had to fight heresy on a number of counts. This is why he begins by emphasizing that when the Christ came, he was a real human being. The three strongest physical senses – sight, hearing and touch – were all used. He says, 'We saw him, we touched him, we heard him.'

For John, the Incarnation is fundamental – ultimately everything boils down to what we think of Jesus. We must realize that he is totally divine and totally human – that in him the physical and the spiritual are totally integrated. The other world and this world have totally met, and the Greek idea that there is a separation between time and eternity, between spiritual and physical, was proven false when the Word became flesh and lived among us. As Archbishop Temple said, 'Christianity is the most materialist of all world religions.'

2. BEHAVIOUR

The Greeks' separation of the physical from the spiritual not only affected their belief about Jesus, but also coloured their behaviour. The Greeks believed that salvation (however this was understood) had nothing to do with what a person did with their body, and this was becoming a normal view inside the church. Some were living quite immoral lives but claiming to be spiritual, because they believed that their body had nothing to do with their soul.

It is a small step from thinking like this to saying that sin doesn't matter in Christians. They say, 'I've got my ticket to heaven – sin doesn't matter.' Indeed, some go even further and say, 'Sin doesn't exist in Christians', suggesting a kind of perfectionism – as far as God is concerned, they are sinless.

One of the biggest mistakes people make when they come to Christ is to think that their future sins are forgiven. But only past sins are forgiven when someone comes to Christ. They need to go on receiving forgiveness for later sins. John has to say, 'If we go on confessing our sins, he is faithful and just to go on forgiving our sins, and the blood of Jesus will go on cleansing us from all unrighteousness.' If I come to Christ, I do not have a blank cheque to sin. My past sins are now forgiven, but I must keep short accounts with God. As I confess them, he goes on forgiving, but only as I go on confessing.

John's emphasis is very much needed in the church today. Greek thinking leads to lawlessness in the church, immorality and spiritual elitism that thinks that Christians are above the normal rules of right and wrong. God is absolutely fair; he doesn't overlook sin in unbelievers or believers. But he is waiting to forgive.

In John's day such teaching wreaked havoc in the church. It left people confused and bewildered, unsure about what they should believe and where they stood with God. They were uncertain about salvation and unconcerned about sin. The teachers seemed to have little regard for the 'ordinary Christians' whom they deemed to be unenlightened.

Assurance

But with great pastoral heart, John is concerned that Christians should be sure that they are Christians, and so he tells them to examine themselves with respect to four areas, and they are quite severe tests. He goes through them very carefully and in great detail.

1. THE DOCTRINAL TEST

The first is the doctrinal test. Every true Christian must pass this test. It concerns how they think of Christ. If someone has a shaky understanding and is not sure if the human Jesus is the divine Christ, they don't pass the test. On 25 occasions in the three letters John uses the verb 'to know'. He believed knowledge was important for the believers, especially in view of the so-called 'higher knowledge' claimed by the Gnostic teachers. There are plenty of people in churches who think of Jesus as a great human being who responded to God better than any other, but they fail to believe that he is fully God and fully man, as the Bible teaches.

2. THE SPIRITUAL TEST

John says, 'We know we are sons of God because he has given us his Spirit.' There is a witness between God's Spirit and our spirit that we are sons of God. So without the Holy Spirit we don't pass the second test, because it's the Spirit who tells us whether we are children of God. Some people try to find assurance from Scripture – they try to deduce that they are Christians from the Bible by arguing that the Bible says it, they believe it, so that settles it. But the Bible never encourages us to do so. Assurance actually comes from the Spirit rather than the Scripture in the New Testament. You can't try to prove you're a Christian by quoting texts. It's the Spirit who tells you that you're a Christian, not the Scriptures. Hence this is a spiritual test, and a crucial one, for if you don't have the Spirit, then you're still a possession of the devil.

3. THE MORAL TEST

The third test is the moral test. If you are living rightly before God, then your conscience tells you that you belong to the Father. Conscience was given as part of our assurance. In biblical terms, if we are practising righteousness and find ourselves keeping the laws of God, then we have a confirmation that we are his children. But if we are rebelling against his laws, and kicking against the way he wants us to live, then we don't pass the third test.

4. THE SOCIAL TEST

The final test is a social test. We are told that we cannot say we love Christ if we don't love Christians, because Christ is in the other Christians. If you love Christ, then you will love the Christ in your brothers. If you hate your brothers, you certainly don't love your Father, because he loves them.

Another proof is the love we have for the Jewish people. They're not lovable. At the human level, I believe I would get on better with Arabs than Jews. But the Spirit can give us a great love for the Jewish people. It's not a natural thing at all, but a supernatural thing. Jesus called them his 'brethren', and God still loves them, in spite of all they've done to him.

In particular, John says that it's our love and our prayers that prove that the love of the Father is in us. You find yourself loving people you would not normally like, because they're children of the Father and the love of the Father is in you.

Once a believer has an assurance of fellowship with God, they have tremendous confidence to set out each day knowing that they are a child of God. This confidence is shown in their attitude towards God. They can say, 'Dad, I am asking you in the name of Jesus for this,' knowing that God is able and willing to respond.

It also gives confidence before men and women. When you are sure you are a child of the royal family of heaven, you are literally part of the royal family on earth, which gives you confidence to speak more boldly to others.

Sin

By the same token, it is also important to identify those who are not real Christians. The church was old enough in John's day to include nominal Christians – people who pretended to be part of God's family but were not actually trusting Christ. One acid test was the presence or absence of sin, and John has a lot to say in his letter about this theme. Indeed, he said some very strange things about this, which seem to contradict one another at times. In some statements he assumes the believers will sin, but in others he says they cannot sin, and this has puzzled many people.

We need to be clear about what John understands by 'sin'. He defines sin as 'lawlessness', meaning that the individual believes he or she is not responsible or accountable to anyone but themselves. John reminds the readers that Christ came to take away our sins and destroy the works of the devil. Sin is normal for the children of the devil, but abnormal for the children of God.

1. THE POSSIBILITIES

But it is the presence of sin within believers that is the biggest concern for John, and this is where the controversy arises. There are a number of possible statements. For believers sin is:

Indisputable – we do sin.
Inevitable – we will sin.
Incompatible – we should not sin.
Intolerable – we must not sin.
Indefensible – we need not sin.
Inapplicable – we do not sin.
Inconceivable – we cannot sin.

The controversy centres on the statements in John's letters that appear to contradict one another. Compare, for example, John's statement in 1 John 1:8 with ones later in the epistle:

If we claim to be without sin, we deceive ourselves and the truth is not in us (1:8).

No-one who is born of God will continue to sin, because God's seed remains in him; he cannot go on sinning, because he has been born of God (3:9).

We know that anyone born of God does not continue to sin; the one who was born of God keeps him safe, and the evil one does not touch him (5:18).

The first verse suggests that sin is inevitable, and the latter two suggest that those who are born of God cannot sin. Yet few would dare to claim that this was true of them. So how should these verses be interpreted?

2. A KEY VERSE EXAMINED

Let's look at the problems with 1 John 3:9.

(a) Major problems

The verse suggests that anyone born of God (i.e. out of water and Spirit, John 3:5) 1. doesn't sin and 2. cannot sin. There are many interpretations:

(i) It is literally true – the verse means exactly what it says. But this would contradict 1:8 and 5:16, which both imply that sin is possible.

(ii) The sin referred to is only crude and blatant sins: vices, crimes and sins against love. Some of the great theologians, such as Augustine, Luther and Wesley, take this view.

(iii) If believers do wrong, God doesn't call it sin. So there are effectively two standards of morality.

(iv) The word only refers to our new nature. The 'old man' still misbehaves, but the 'new man' never does. However, a Christian is not a divided person, but a unity!

(v) The verse describes the ideal, without ever believing that it is actually possible. So this reflects a goal we are to desire, without ever imagining that we will achieve it.

(vi) The verse only refers to habitual, persistent sin. The tense suggests someone who goes on sinning.

(b) Minor problems

(i)   The reason the believer doesn't sin is that they are 'born of God'. Regeneration is said to lead to righteousness. But who would claim to be righteous this side of heaven?

(ii) Secondly, we are told that God's seed remains in the believer. The word literally means 'sperm', which is a very potent metaphor! But how should the word be interpreted? It can be used literally as referring to human sperm, or even animal or vegetable sperm. But it is not clear what 'his seed' refers to. Does it refer to God or the believer?

(iii) Then there's a third problem. Is this a categorical statement or a conditional statement? The use of the phrase 'abide/remain in Christ' also seems open to interpretation. Is this categorical as in verse 9, true of everyone who was once 'born of God'? Or is it conditional as in verse 6, true only of those who '*live* in him'? A categorical statement is a statement that will always be true. A conditional statement is one that will be true, if certain conditions follow.

How then should we understand the verse?

First, we need to ask why John is making this statement. He is not discussing the 'once saved, always saved' conundrum. He is dealing with those who call themselves disciples, but continue to sin and accept it, almost as if it doesn't matter!

So John says we can't sin because we are born of God. The clear implication is that regeneration leads to righteousness. Sin has no place in the believer's life.

Secondly, we should note the tense of 'no one who lives in him keeps on sinning.' The verbs here are in a special Greek tense called the continuous present. So the verbs don't just refer to something done at the time, but something you continue doing.

So, for example, Jesus didn't actually say 'Ask, and you'll receive; seek, and you'll find; knock, and the door will be opened.' He said, 'Keep on asking, and you will receive; keep on seeking, and you will find; keep on knocking, and the door will be opened.' Take the famous verse, John 3:16, which is generally totally misunderstood. This is also in the present continuous tense: 'For God so loved the world that he gave his only-begotten Son, that whoever goes on believing in him will never perish but will go on having eternal life.' It is not that those who believe once have eternal life, but it's those who go on believing who go on having life.

So to return to this verse, it says, 'No one who goes on living in Christ will go on sinning.' The word 'lives' is the same as the word 'abides'. John 15 says: 'I am the true vine – remain in me', which means 'stay in me', 'go on living in me'. The verse is therefore conditioned by the context. You go on living in Christ, and the statement then becomes true. Whoever goes on living in Christ doesn't go on sinning and can't go on sinning.

People who are not continuing in Christ will not show any progress spiritually. They will not be moving into this promise.

The third verse quoted earlier (1 John 5:18) backs this up: 'We know that anyone born of God does not continue to sin; the one who was born of God keeps him safe, and the evil one does not touch him.'

So whoever is born of God 'does not continue to sin' – they cannot go on sinning, because if they're living in Christ they will make progress and will have victory. It's the relationship with Christ that determines the truth of this promise. This whole letter assumes that Christians will fall into sin – there will be no one perfect this side of heaven – but not that they will go on sinning.

For our understanding we must add the perspective of the Letter to the Hebrews, which says that if you receive forgiveness but deliberately go on sinning, there remains no more sacrifice for sin. It's not saying Christians will never sin but that they have a way of dealing with it, and if they are living in Christ they will want to deal with it. One of the proofs that you're a Christian is that when you sin you hate it. You don't love sin and you want to be rid of it. Those who go on living in Christ cannot go on sinning. It is incompatible with the new life within.

Having dealt with this problem, chapter 5 suggests something else which is very serious. We are told that when we see a brother sinning, we should do everything we can to help him and convert him from his evil ways. If we do, we have 'saved' a brother. But, John adds, there is a 'sin unto death'. There is no point in praying for a brother who's sinned unto death!

All the way through Scripture we find that backsliders can reach a point of no return. There is a sin unto death, and we need to take these warnings very seriously. They are most prominent in the Letter to the Hebrews. There comes a point where repentance is impossible. John says that a brother can so sin that it's no use praying for him any more. This means, of course, that he is not living in Christ, that he has lost his link with the true vine, and is no longer abiding.

So if we synthesize all that John says about sin and believers, we will have a beautiful balance. We will not become neurotic on the one hand or complacent on the other. There will be a healthy fear of the Lord that will keep us in Christ. But if we take just one verse out of its context, we can create havoc.

God

In the light of his concerns about sin, John wants his readers to understand what God is like. He reminds them that God is 'light' – God is pure and holy and morally separate from the world. God is also 'life'. Sin leads to death, but life comes from God – it is his gift to us. The God whom John describes wants fellowship with us. The word 'fellowship' literally means 'sharing' or 'partnership'. John explains the conditions for fellowship with such a God:

1. WALK IN LIGHT

We must embrace the light and shun the darkness. We cannot have fellowship with God or his people if we have hidden lives – our lives should be transparent.

2. WALK IN LOVE

The imperative is to love God and our new brothers. Indeed, if we don't love them, we can't love him – it's as simple as that. The command to love one another is described as an 'old command', even though Jesus described it as a 'new commandment'. The reason is simple – it was now 60 years since it was first given.

3. WALK IN LIFE

Christ has provided all that is necessary for living the new life; therefore the believers are encouraged to live in the good of it.

It is clear that John's passion is that the readers might experience the joy of fellowship with Christ, and that nothing should get in the way of that.

2 and 3 John

Introduction

For our study of these two letters, we are going to look first at the difference between men and women. It may seem an unusual way to begin, but it provides a helpful foundation for grasping the outline and purpose of each book. When God made us in his image, he made us male and female, and therefore complementary to one another. It's astonishing how the strengths of maleness correspond to the weaknesses of female-ness, and vice versa. We need each other.

The diagram overleaf looks at the difference between men and women – that is, between the average man, represented by one circle, and the average woman, represented by the other – though, clearly, there will be men and women who show these characteristics to a greater or lesser measure. There are effeminate men and masculine women.

The humanist tends to assume that there is just one spectrum – a male end and a female end, with a mixture in the middle, as if we're all really one. But we are separately male and female, and the two spectrums overlap.

This helps us to understand the differences between 2 John and 3 John. 2 John is the only letter in the New Testament addressed to a woman, and 3 John is an almost identical letter addressed to a man. They say opposite things and yet they have the same subject.

The obvious visual difference is that men are angular to look at while women are curved. Men have an analytical brain, whereas women are more intuitive. It's quite irritating when my wife comes to the same conclusion as myself, especially when she reaches it six weeks earlier! Intuition is much stronger in most women, whereas men like to sit down and think it through.

Men can think in more abstract terms, and women can think in more concrete terms. Men think of general things, women think of particular things. So whereas men are goal-orientated and live for the future, women are need-orientated. A man is fulfilled if he has a goal to aim for; a woman is fulfilled if she has a need to meet. Men therefore tend to be more interested in things and women tend to be more interested in people.

This is reflected in conversation. A male gathering is likely to talk about motorbikes and cars, whereas women will get together and talk about people and relationships.

ALL

AVERAGE MALE

MALES

TALLER
ANGULAR
ANALYTICAL
GOAL-ORIENTED
ABSTRACT
GENERAL
THINGS
TRUTH

MASCULINE
EFFEMINATE

ALL

AVERAGE FEMALE

FEMALES

SHORTER
CURVED
INTUITIVE
NEED-ORIENTED
CONCRETE
PARTICULAR
PEOPLE
LOVE

A man can separate his thoughts from his feelings, whereas a woman thinks as a whole person. This is why a man can be in love with more than one woman at once, but a woman can generally only be in love with one man. Women need to understand that men face different temptations for this reason. If a wife finds that her husband has gone off with a woman at the office, she will assume he doesn't love her any more. His claims that he does still love her aren't understood because of this difference.

This ability to be cold and analytical is one reason why men have a particular responsibility for discipline. They can separate their feelings from their thoughts and be more objective about a situation that needs confronting and punishing. I happen to believe in capital punishment. People ask whether I could press the button. I reply that I think I could, but I would never ask my wife to.

It's because of these differences that men are more concerned with truth and women with love. But the danger of men is to have too much emphasis on truth and too little on love, and the danger of women is to have too little emphasis on truth and too much on love. John's second and third epistles perfectly fit this pattern. They are very similar, but the differences correspond to these gender characteristics.

An outline of 2 and 3 John

2 JOHN	3 JOHN
♀	♂

HOSPITALITY – TRUTH AND LOVE

To a lady	To a man
Danger:	Danger:
too much love	too much truth
Attitude:	Attitude:
too soft-hearted	too hard-headed
Door open too wide	Door shut too tightly
Welcome wrong people	Refuse right people
Neglect truth	Neglect love
Wrong belief	Wrong behaviour

We need both ...

Female	Male
Love	Truth
Love *and* truth	Truth *and* love
in women	in men

The letters are very short. They would each have fitted onto one sheet of papyrus, probably A4 size. They are both concerned with the subject of hospitality and were probably written together.

Hospitality was especially important in the early church because Christians weren't by and large welcome anywhere else. There were no church buildings, and so they met in each other's homes. Futhermore, the inns often doubled as brothels, so they weren't suitable for travelling preachers. Most would have depended upon believers for financial support.

The church needs both travelling ministries and local ministries. Some churches are locked into their own local ministry and don't listen enough to other ministries. Others live on visiting preachers all the time, but don't have enough of their own. But in the New Testament there were local ministries – pastors and teachers – and travelling ministries – apostles, prophets and evangelists. One of the earliest Christian writings, The Didache, warns that if a prophet stays more than three days with you, he's a false prophet. Prophets get too intense if they're permanent. If you have a resident prophet, then you are in trouble, because they come on heavy week after week!

Prophets and evangelists need to travel; pastors and teachers need to stay put. Servants of the church need to choose whether they prefer to be the pastor of a church or a travelling preacher. It's unfair on a church if they try to do both. I've seen many churches wrecked because they never knew whether the pastor would be there or not.

John writes these two letters because he believes the attitude to hospitality has been inappropriate. Each reflects the weakness common to their gender – the lady was throwing the door open too wide and the man was keeping it too tightly shut. They represent the typical responses that we can learn from.

The lady's danger was that she had too much love and not enough truth. She was welcoming people she ought not to have welcomed. She was giving hospitality, but her attitude was that she was too soft-hearted and accommodating to anyone who wanted to stay. She was unwittingly being used to introduce bad teaching to the church. John had to rebuke her mildly that in doing this she was neglecting the truth.

Many heresies have been promoted within the church through women. The woman's heart goes with the teacher, but she needs to spend time evaluating the teaching as well. Paul's second letter to Timothy shows us that heretical teachers were especially successful in deceiving widows and weak-willed women. Paul had to urge Timothy to protect them from being misled. This is one reason why Paul tells Timothy that women should not be involved in teaching. He points out that Eve was deceived, though we must add that Eve was fooled in the presence of Adam, who kept his mouth shut.

The opposite danger is found in John's third letter. He is writing about a man who is too jealous for his own ministry and not welcoming to any other teacher. Good teachers were being refused entrance who could bring some real help to the fellowship. His danger is that he's so focused on truth that he's forgotten love. He thinks he has everything 100 per cent doctrinally correct and nobody else has. So he shuts the door, and his attitude is too hard-hearted.

The two letters emphasize the importance of teamwork between men and women. God made us for each other, though it doesn't mean we can only find this partnership in marriage. Jesus is a perfect example of a single man who had perfect relationships with women. He appreciated them, ministered to them and allowed them to minister to him. But he still made clear distinctions between the roles and responsibilities of men and women. Both are equally made in the image of God and are equal in dignity, depravity and destiny. We need love and truth in the woman, and we need truth and love in the man.

An analysis of 2 and 3 John

	2 John		3 John
1–3	Love in truth	1	Love in truth
4	Following truth	2–4	Following truth
5–6	Following love	5–8	Following love
7–9	Some reject truth	9–10	Some refuse love
10–11	Don't invite them	11–12	Don't imitate them
12–13	Our joy	13–15	Your peace

These letters were clearly written at the same time and follow exactly the same pattern. The 'second' letter is addressed to Kyria, which means 'lady', but we don't know if this is the title of a prominent lady or not. The 'children' referred to could be the spiritual children who meet in her home. The analysis shows that the same outline is followed in each letter, and yet the emphasis for the man and the woman is totally different.

The 'third' letter is addressed to Gaius, but contains a warning about a man called Diotrephes. The description of him is not positive. He was a man guilty of being too tight. He was talkative, over-bearing, headstrong and power-hungry. He was jealous for his little fellowship and didn't want other teachers coming in and distracting people away from his leadership. He refused to allow the apostle John to visit, even tearing up a letter he had written.

Here was a man who excommunicated anyone not on his side and who was malicious against those who didn't agree with him – even the apostles. There is no record that he was not orthodox in his beliefs, but he was certainly stifling the teaching gifts that others would bring.

So John had to urge Gaius to welcome Demetrius – a respected teacher who shouldn't have been turned away. It is not clear whether Demetrius was a local or travelling preacher. He may even have been the postman who took the letters to the church. He was certainly known to them.

The elderly apostle

There are two stories about John in his old age which we know from church records. They reveal John's balance of truth and love. He stood firmly for the truth, refusing to compromise, especially concerning the Person of Christ. But at the same time he was the most loving old man.

An early church writer, Jerome, tells a story about John from the AD 90s. By this time John was very old, and used to be carried into church every week on a chair with poles through it. The church members would often ask him to speak. He would sit in the chair at the front and he'd just say, 'Little children, love one another!'

The next Sunday they would carry him into church and ask if he had a word for them. 'Yes,' he'd say, 'I've got a word for you today.' They would carry the chair to the front and he'd say, 'Little children, love one another!'

The next Sunday they brought him in and exactly the same thing happened. They began to think he was getting senile. Didn't he realize that he kept repeating the same words? They finally went to the old man and said, 'Master, why do you always say, "Little children, love one another"?' He said: 'Because it is the Lord's command, and if this only is done, it is enough.'

Another tale demonstrates that John's concern for truth was no less strong. He made frequent visits to the Roman baths to bathe. Once he was lowered into the water, and at the other end of the pool he saw a man called Cerinthus. He was the leading false teacher who was going round the churches. John said, 'Let us fly! let us fly! lest even the bath-house fall down because Cerinthus, the enemy of the truth, is within!'

So they had to lift him out and take him home unwashed that day. John was the most loving man, but truth was all-important too.

When Jesus met him he was one of the most bad-tempered men around. Jesus called John and his brother James 'Boanerges', which meant 'sons of thunder' – not a flattering nickname! John's reaction to the Samaritans was not untypical. When the Samaritans spat on them as they walked through Samaria, he said, 'I'm going to call fire down from heaven, if you give me permission, Jesus, and we'll burn up the whole lot of them!'

Later on he and James were persuaded by their mother to request a higher position than the other apostles when Jesus entered his Kingdom.

Some suggest that his later, milder manner came because he mellowed with age. But not everyone mellows with age! This was the man whom Jesus loved, and bit by bit his character was made like his Master's.

These letters display none of the less pleasant characteristics of a former period in his life. Here is a man who is now full of love and truth, and longs that others should be too. Jesus has changed him, and he is concerned in these letters that his readers should come to know and value the Saviour in the way that he does.

PART VI

REVELATION

Differences of opinion

Opinions about the Book of Revelation cover a huge spectrum. When put together, it seems impossible that they all refer to the same piece of literature.

Human Opinion

Human opinion varies enormously. The reaction of unbelievers is understandable, since it is not intended for them. It is probably the worst book to use as an introduction to Christian Scriptures. The world assumes it is the result of 'indigestion at best or insanity at worst', to quote a typical comment.

Yet even among Christians there are diverse attitudes, ranging from the fearful who can't get into the book to the fanatical who can't get out of it! Bible scholars have made many negative comments: 'as many riddles as there are words'; 'haphazard accumulation of weird symbols'; 'either finds a man mad or leaves him mad'.

Surprisingly, most of the Protestant Reformers (the 'magisterial' ones, so called because they used the civic authorities to achieve their objectives) had an extremely low view:

Luther: 'neither apostolic nor prophetic ... everyone thinks of the book whatever his spirit suggests ... there are many nobler books to be retained ... my spirit cannot acquiesce in this book.'

Calvin: omitted it from his New Testament commentary!

Zwingli: said its testimony can be rejected because 'it is not a book of the Bible'.

This down-grading has influenced many denominations which sprang from the Reformation.

There had, as we know, been some debate in the early Church about its inclusion in the 'canon' (rule or standard) of Scripture; but by the fifth century it was confidently and universally included.

Some commentators are very positive in their assessment: 'the only masterpiece of pure art in the New Testament; 'beautiful beyond description'. Even William Barclay, who collected these varied comments but was himself inclined to a 'liberal' view of Scripture, told his readers that it was 'infinitely worthwhile to wrestle with it until it gives its blessings and opens its riches'.

Satanic opinion

Satanic opinion is consistently negative. The devil hates the first few pages of the Bible (which reveal how he gained control of our planet) and the last few pages (which reveal how he will lose control of it). If he can convince humans that Genesis is composed of impossible myths and Revelation of impenetrable mysteries, he is content.

The author has remarkable proof of Satan's particular hatred of Revelation 20. Many cassette recordings of an exposition of this chapter have been damaged between despatch and receipt. In some cases the section dealing with the devil's doom has been wiped clean before reaching its destination; in others a screaming voice using a foreign language has been superimposed, rendering the original words unintelligible!

The book calls his bluff. He is only prince and ruler of this world by God's permission. And that has only been given temporarily.

Divine opinion

Divine opinion is consistently positive. It is the only book in the Bible to which divine sanctions of reward and punishment have been directly attached. On the one hand, a special blessing will rest upon those who read it aloud, both to themselves and others (1:3) and who 'keep the words', by meditation and application (22:7). On the other, a special curse will rest on those who tamper with its text. If this is done by addition, or by insertions, the plagues described in the book will be added to the culprit's experience. If it is done by subtraction, by deletions, the culprit's share of eternal life in the new Jerusalem will be taken away.

Such a blessing and curse tell us how seriously God regards the facts and truths revealed here. He could hardly have made its importance clearer.

From these opinions about the book, we turn to look at the book itself.

Consider first its position in the Bible. Just as Genesis could be nowhere else but at the beginning, Revelation could be nowhere else but at the end. In so many ways it completes the 'story'.

If the Bible is simply regarded as the history of our world, Revelation is needed to round it off. Of course, biblical history is different from all other such publications. It starts earlier, before there were any observers to record events. It finishes later, by predicting events that cannot yet be observed and recorded.

This, of course, raises the question as to whether we are dealing with works of human imagination or divine inspiration. The answer depends on faith. It is a simple choice: to believe or not to believe. While going beyond reason, faith is not contrary to reason. The biblical accounts of the origin and destiny of our universe can be shown to be the best explanation of its present state. To know how it will end is of profound significance to the way we live now.

But the interest of the Bible is in the human race rather than the environment and in God's chosen people in particular. With them he has a 'covenant' relationship, analogous to marriage. From one point of view, the Bible is the story of a romance, a heavenly Father seeking an earthly bride for his Son. Like every good romance, they 'get married and live happily ever after'. But this climax is only reached in the Book of Revelation, without which we would never know whether the engagement (or 'betrothal'; 2 Corinthians 11:2) ever came to anything or was broken off!

Indeed, it is quite difficult to imagine what it would be like to have a Bible without the Book of Revelation, even if we don't use it much. Imagine a New Testament that closed with the little Letter of Jude addressed to a second-generation church that was being corrupted in its creed, conduct, character and conversation. So is that how it will all end? What a depressing anticlimax!

So most Christians are glad that the Book of Revelation is there, even if they are not very well acquainted with it. They can usually cope with the first few chapters and the last few, but feel out of their depth in the central bulk of it (chapters 6–18). That is largely because this portion is so unlike anything else. It is difficult because it is different. Just what makes it so?

The nature of apocalyptic writing

Revelation is not only different from other New Testament books in content. It is also unique in origin.

All the others were intended to be written. Each author decided to put pen to paper, either himself or through an 'amanuensis' (i.e. a secretary; e.g. Romans 16:22). He considered what he wanted to say before it was put down. The result bore the marks of his own temperament, character, outlook and experience – even though he was 'inspired' by the Holy Spirit, prompting his thoughts and feelings.

Scholars have noted many differences between Revelation and the other writings of the apostle John (one Gospel and three Epistles). The style, grammar and vocabulary are so unusual for him that they have concluded that it must come from another 'John'. They have actually found a somewhat vague reference to an obscure elder of that name in Ephesus to fit the bill. But the man who wrote Revelation simply introduces himself as 'I, John' (1:9), which indicates that he was well and widely known.

There is a simpler explanation for the contrast, even apart from the obvious difference of subject. He never intended to write Revelation. He never even thought about it. It came to him as a totally unexpected 'revelation' in verbal annd visual form. As he 'heard' and 'saw' this astonishing series of voices and visions, he was repeatedly told to 'write' it all down (1:11, 19; 2:1, 8, 12, 18; 3:1; 7:14; 14:13; 19:9; 21:5). The reiterated command suggests that he became so absorbed in what was happening to him that he forgot to record it from time to time.

This explains the 'inferior Greek', compared to his normal fluency. It was written hurriedly in very distracting circumstances. Imagine watching a film and being told to 'get it all down on paper', while it was being shown. College students

will understand the 'scrappy' style by looking at their lecture
notes. Why, then, did John not write it up afterwards from his
scribbled précis, so that its permanent form might be rather
more polished? He was hardly likely to when the last dictated
words contained a curse on anyone who tampered with what
he had written!

All this means that John was not the author of Revelation.
He was merely the 'amanuensis' who took it down. So who was
the 'author'? The message was often communicated to him
by angels. But it was also what the Spirit was saying to the
churches; and it was the revelation of Jesus Christ. But it was
given to Jesus by God. So a complex chain of communication
was involved – God, Jesus, Spirit, angels, John. More than
once, poor John was confused about who should get the glory
for what he was experiencing (19:10; 22:8–9). Only the first
two links in the chain are worshipped in this book.

More directly than any other book in the New Testament,
this deserves the name of 'Revelation'. The Greek word so
translated in the first sentence is *apokalypsis*, from which came
the noun 'Apocalypse' and the adjective 'apocalyptic', which is
now more widely used of other literature similar in style and
content. The root word means 'unveiling'.

It is the pulling back of a curtain to reveal what has been
hidden (as in the unveiling of a picture or plaque).

In the context of Scripture, it is the unveiling of that which
is hidden from man, but is known to God. There are some
things which man cannot know unless God chooses to inform
him. In particular, he cannot know what is happening in heaven
and he cannot know what will happen in the future. His
recording and interpreting of events is therefore strictly limited
in both time and space. It can only be, at best, a partial account
of the flow of history.

When God writes history, he gives a total picture, not least because he orders as well as observes the events. 'History is his story.' He 'makes known the end from the beginning, from ancient times, what is still to come' (Isaiah 46:10). Past, present and future are interrelated in him.

So are heaven and earth. There is an interaction between what goes on up there and what goes on down here. One of the disturbing features in Revelation is the constant shift of scene from earth to heaven and back again. That is because of the connection between events above and below (e.g. war in heaven leads to war on earth; 12:7; 13:7).

'Apocalyptic' is history written from God's point of view. It gives the total picture. It enlarges our understanding of world events by seeing them in the light of what is above and beyond our limited perception. This gives us both insight and foresight, enlarging our comprehension of what is going on around us, far beyond that of the normal historian.

Patterns and purposes emerge to which he is blind. History is not just a haphazard accumulation of happenings. Coincidence gives way to providence. History is going somewhere.

Time is eternally significant. Time and eternity are interrelated. God is not outside time, as Greek philosophy imagined. He is inside time; or rather, time is inside God. He is the God who was, is and is to come. Even God himself cannot change the past, once it has happened! The death and resurrection of Jesus can never be changed or cancelled.

God is working out his plans and purposes within time (the classic book on this is *Christ and Time* by Oscar Cullmann, SCM Press, 1950). He is the Lord of history. But it is his pattern, which can only be discerned when he has revealed the missing pieces of the jigsaw. Things hidden from human observation and which God reveals are called 'mysteries' in the New Testament.

The direction of events in the past and present becomes apparent in the light of the future. The shape of history cannot be seen in the short term, only in the long term. For time is relative as well as real to God. 'A thousand years are like a day' to him (Psalm 90:4, quoted in 2 Peter 3:8). His amazing patience with us makes him appear 'slow' to us (2 Peter 3:9).

The Bible contains a 'philosophy of history' quite different from those which man's unaided reason has adopted. The contrast is clear when we compare it with the four most commonly held ideas:

1. *Cyclic.* 'History repeats itself'. It simply goes round in endless circles, or cycles. Sometimes the world gets better, then worse, then better, then worse again … and so on. This was the Greek idea.

2. *Rhythmic.* This is a variation on the cyclic. The world still alternates between better and worse, but never repeats itself in exactly the same way. It is always moving on, but whether it will end on an 'up' or a 'down' is anyone's guess!

3. *Optimistic.* The world is getting better and better. As one British Prime Minister said at the beginning of the twentieth century: 'up and up and up and on and on and on'. The word on everyone's lips then was 'progress'. History was an ascending escalator.

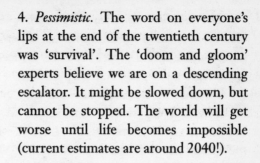

4. *Pessimistic.* The word on everyone's lips at the end of the twentieth century was 'survival'. The 'doom and gloom' experts believe we are on a descending escalator. It might be slowed down, but cannot be stopped. The world will get worse until life becomes impossible (current estimates are around 2040!).

The biblical pattern is quite different from all of these, combining both pessimism and optimism in a realism based on all the facts.

5. *Apocalyptic.* The world will get steadily worse, then suddenly better than it has ever been – and will stay that way.

This last belief is shared by Jews, Christians and Communists. They all got it from the same source: the Hebrew prophets (Karl Marx had a Jewish mother and a Lutheran father). The basic difference between them is what they believe will bring about the sharp change of direction. Communists believe it will be by human revolution. Jews believe it will be by divine intervention. Christians believe it will be by the return of the God-man Jesus to planet earth.

Those who have read through the book of Revelation will now realize that it is actually structured on this very basis. After dealing with the present in its earlier chapters, it turns to the future course of history, which gets steadily worse (in chapters 6–18), then suddenly better (in chapters 20–22), the change coinciding with the Second Coming of Christ (in chapter 19).

There are two more characteristics of 'apocalyptic' history that we must talk about before moving on.

The first feature is that the pattern is basically *moral*. Since history is ordered by God and he is perfectly good and all-powerful, we would expect to see his justice administered in the encouragment of good and the punishment of evil.

But this does not seem to be the case, either in international or individual experience. Life seems to be terribly unjust. History seems indifferent to morality. The righteous suffer and the wicked prosper. The constant cry is: 'Why does a good God allow such things to go on?' The Bible is honest enough to record the bewilderment of Job, David (Psalm 73:1–4), Jesus himself (Mark 15:34, the words of Psalm 22:1), and the Christians who were martyred for him (Revelation 6:10).

All such doubts spring from a short-term view focused mainly on the present and partly on the past. A long-term view takes the future, the ultimate outcome, into account. This can totally change the understanding (Job 42; Psalm 73:15–28; Hebrews 12:2; Revelation 20:4; Paul sums it up in Romans 8:18).

'Apocalyptic' portions of the Bible all encourage this long-term view which reveals that history does uphold morality (Daniel 7–12, with which Revelation has much in common, is an excellent example). We do live in a moral universe. The good God is still on the throne. He will bring it all to the right conclusion. He will punish the wicked and reward the righteous. He will put the world right again and give it to those who have been willing to be put right themselves. There will be a 'happy ever after' ending to the story.

'Apocalyptic' literature, including Revelation, therefore concentrates on such themes as reward, retribution and restoration. Above all, it pictures God reigning on a throne, in perfect control of world affairs. Notice that word 'pictures', which introduces the other quality.

The second feature is that the presentation is often *symbolical*. It has to be, since the unfamiliar is being communicated. As every teacher knows, the unknown has somehow to be related to the known, usually by analogy ('well, it's like this'). Most of Jesus' parables about the Kingdom of Heaven use earthly situations to assist understanding ('the Kingdom of Heaven is like …').

Helping people to comprehend something involves imagination as much as information. If they can 'picture' it in their mind, it will be much easier to grasp. Significantly, the response is usually: 'Now I see'.

Revelation is full of pictorial language. Through the constant use of 'symbols' we can visualize what would otherwise be incomprehensible. It cannot be too strongly emphasized that this is intended to help our understanding, not hinder it. Too many have used the 'highly symbolic' nature of the book to ignore or even dismiss its teaching, as if the symbols are too obscure to convey a clear message. That is simply not the case, as is apparent when they are listed in four categories:

Some are *obvious* in their meaning. The 'dragon' or 'serpent' is the devil. The 'lake of fire' is hell. The 'great white throne' is the Lord's judgement seat.

Some are *explained* in the context. The 'stars' are angels. The 'lampstands' are churches. The 'seals', 'trumpets' and 'bowls' are disasters. The 'incense' represents prayers ascending. The 'ten horns' are kings.

Some are *paralleled* elsewhere in scripture. In the Old Testament may be found the tree of life, the rainbow, the morning star, the rod of iron, horsemen, tyrannical regimes pictured as wild 'beasts'. It may safely be assumed that these emblems have retained their original meaning.

Some are *obscure*, but very few. One example is the 'white stone', for which scholars have offered an amazing number of interpretations. A declaration of innocence? A sign of approval? A badge of excellence? Maybe we won't know what it signifies until we receive one!

Numbers are also used as symbols. There are many 'sevens' in Revelation – stars, lampstands, lamps, seals, trumpets, bowls. It is the 'round' number of the Bible, the complete, the perfect figure. 'Twelve' is associated with the old people of God (their tribes) and the new (their apostles); 'twenty-four' brings them together. 'One thousand' is the largest number. 'Twelve thousand' from each tribe of Israel brings the total to 'one hundred and forty-four thousand'.

'666' is the one that captures attention. It is made up of sixes, a figure which always points to the human failure to reach the seven of 'complete perfection'. It is used here as a clue to the identity of the last world dictator before Jesus reigns for a thousand years (in Latin, a *millennium*). Is it significant that '666' is the total of all the Roman numerals (I=1 + V=5 + X=10 + L=50 +C=100 + D=500) except one (M=1000)? But all attempts to name him from this figure will fail until his appearing makes it perfectly clear.

There is so much in Revelation that is quite clear that we can cope with a few obscurities now, believing that they will be clarified by future events when the information is really needed. Meanwhile, we can thank God that he has told us so much.

Of course, he speaks through human voices, through the mouths of his 'prophets'. John realized that the message he delivered was not his. He calls his writing 'this prophecy' (1:3; 22:7, 10, 18, 19). He is therefore a prophet as well as an apostle. This is the only 'prophetic' book in the New Testament.

Prophecy is both 'forthtelling' (a word of God about the present) and 'foretelling' (a word of God about the future). Revelation is both, the greater part being predictions of events yet to happen.

When will they be fulfilled? Have they happened already? Are they happening right now? Or have they still to happen? We must now consider the various answers being given to these questions.

Schools of interpretation

Nearly one third of the verses in the book of Revelation contain a prediction. Between them, some 56 separate events are foretold. Exactly half of these are in plain language and the other half are in symbolic picture form.

Most of them occur after chapter 4, which opens with a marked change in perspective – from earth to heaven and from present to future ('come up here and I will show you what must take place after this'; 4:1).

Clearly, this refers to happenings that are future to the original writer and readers in the first century AD. But how far ahead of them did the forecast stretch? Are the predicted events past, present or future to us who live 19 centuries later? Do we look behind, around or ahead for their fulfilment?

This is where the differences begin. Over the intervening years between then and now, four major opinions have arisen, leading to four 'schools of interpretation'. Most commentaries are written from only one point of view. It is important to look at them all before assuming that one is right. It is too easy and risky to follow the first that has been heard or read about.

The four are now so well established, they have been given familiar labels: preterist, historicist (of which there are two distinct varieties), futurist and idealist. Don't be put off by this rather technical jargon. It is important to be able to identify the very different approaches you may encounter.

1. Preterist

This school regards the predictions as fulfilled during the decline and fall of the Roman Empire, when the church was under the pressures of imperial persecutions. It was written for Christians of the first century, to prepare them for what would happen in the second and third. The 'great city' of Babylon, sitting on 'seven hills' (17:9) is identified as Rome (Peter seems to make the same comparison; 1 Peter 5:13).

Though the bulk of Revelation is thus 'past' to us, that does not mean it is of limited value. We can learn lessons from all the historical narrative in scripture. Indeed, it constitutes the major part of the Bible. We can draw inspiration and instruction from what has gone before.

The strength of this view is that all Bible study should begin with the original context of writer and readers. What did this mean to them? What the writer intended and what the readers would understand in their situation are vital steps towards a true interpretation and application.

But there are a number of weaknesses. For one thing, very few if any of the specific predictions actually came true in the Roman Empire. Only a few general trends can be identified but no particular correspondence (some have tried to distil '666' from the letters of 'Nero Caesar', though Revelation was probably written 30 years after his death!). It also means that after Rome fell, the major part of the book lost its direct relevance and really said little to the later church. Since nearly all scholars accept that the last few chapters cover the end of the world, which is still future to us, a huge gap is left between the beginning and end of church history, with no direct guidance for the many intervening centuries. This deficiency is met by the second approach.

2. Historicist

This school believes the predictions cover the entire 'church age' between the First and Second Comings of Christ. It is a coded history of 'anno domini' in symbolic form, covering the major phases and crises of the entire period. So the fulfilment is past, present and future to us. We are right in there and from what has already come to pass we can know what is next on the programme.

One scholar produced a cross-reference index between every section of Revelation and the many volumes of the *Cambridge Ancient and Modern History*. It is generally held that we are living somewhere in chapter 16 or 17!

At least this theory has made the book relevant to every generation of Christians. It has also stimulated interest. But this is more than outweighed by its drawbacks.

One is that many details are rather forced to fit known events, which appears somewhat artificial. But the main problem is that no two 'historicists' seem to agree on the correlation of Scripture and history! Were they using the right method, there would surely be a greater degree of unanimity in their conclusions. And they still finish up with many unfulfilled details.

So far we have only considered one type of 'historicism'. We will call it *linear*, because it believes that the central part of Revelation goes in one straight line of events from the first to the Second Advent of Christ.

There is another type, which we will call the *cyclical*, which believes that it covers the whole church history more than once, constantly returning to the beginning and 'recapitulating' the events from another angle. One popular volume (*More than Conquerors* by William Hendiksen, Baker, 1960) claims to have discovered seven such cycles, each covering the whole church age (in chapters 1–3, 4–7, 8–11, 12–14, 15–16, 17–19, 20–22)! This enables him to place the 'Millennium' (in chapter 20) before the Second Coming (chapter 19) and therefore hold the 'post-millennial' view. But this 'progressive parallelism', as it is called, seems to be forced onto the text, rather than found within it. In particular, the radical separation of chapters 19 and 20 is totally unwarranted.

The historicist interpretation is probably the least satisfactory and the least convincing, in either linear or cyclical form.

3. Futurist

This school believes that the central block of predictions applies to the last few years leading up to the Second Coming. It is therefore still future to us today, hence the label. It concerns the climax of evil control in the world, which will be the 'Great Tribulation' for the people of God (Revelation 7:14; also referred to by Jesus in Matthew 24:12–22).

All the events will be compressed into quite a short time – three and a half years, to be exact (explicitly referred to as 'a time, times and half a time' or 'forty-two months' or 'one thousand, two hundred and sixty days'; 11:2–3; 12:6, 14, quoting Daniel 12:7).

Since the events are still future, the predictions tend to be taken more literally, as an accurate description of what will happen. There is no longer any need to tailor them to fit past history. Certainly, the series of disasters seems to lead straight into the end of the world.

What, then, is the message for the church through the ages? Most of the book would only be relevant to the very last generation of believers in this case. Surprisingly, many futurists also believe that the church will be 'raptured' to heaven before the troubles start, so even the last Christians don't need to know these things either!

A further weakness is that futurists are prone to treat Revelation as an 'almanac', leading to an excessive interest in charts, schedules of the future. The fact that they do not always agree suggests that Revelation was not primarily written for such speculative purposes.

4. Idealist

This approach removes all specific time references and discourages correlation with particular events. Revelation pictures the 'eternal' struggle between good and evil and the 'truths' contained in its narratives can be applied to any century. The battle between God and Satan is ongoing, but the divine victory can be experienced by an 'overcoming' church at any time. The 'essential message' can be universally applied throughout time and space.

The main and perhaps only merit of this view is that the message of the book becomes directly relevant to all who read it. They are in the struggle that is described and are assured that 'the one who is in you is greater than the one who is in the world' (1 John 4:4). It is possible to be 'more than conquerors' (Romans 8:37).

This, however, is to treat Revelation as 'myth'. It is spiritually true, but not historically true. These are fictional events, but the stories contain truths – as in Aesop's fables or *Pilgrim's Progress*. The truths must be dug out of the narrative before being applied. The cost of this 'demythologizing' process is to jettison a great deal of material, dismissing it as poetic licence which belongs to the package rather than the content.

Behind all this is the Greek philosophy which separated spiritual and physical, sacred and secular, eternity and time. God, they said, is timeless. So truth is timeless, though it is also therefore timely. But it is not in 'the times'. Their notion of history as cyclical cut out the concept of the 'end-time', the idea that time would reach a climax or conclusion.

This has serious consequences for 'eschatology' (the study of 'the last things', from the Greek word *eschatos* = 'end' or 'last'). Events like the Second Coming and the Day of Judgement are transferred from the future to the present, from then to now. Eschatology becomes 'existential' (i.e. concerned with the present moment of existence, or it is said to be 'realized' (as in 'realizing investments' – having the money to spend now).

Of course, radical changes have to be made to the 'predictions' to make them fit the present – usually by 'spiritualizing' them (a 'Platonic' way of thinking). For example, the 'New Jerusalem' (in chapter 21) becomes the description of a people rather than a place, an 'idealized' (note the word) picture of the church, the architectural details conveniently forgotten!

It is time to summarize this survey. There are four different answers to the question: what period of time does Revelation cover?

The preterist replies: the first few centuries AD.

The historicist replies: all the centuries AD from the First to the Second Advent.

The futurist replies: the last years of the last century AD.

The idealist replies: any century AD, none in particular.

So which is right? There are pros and cons for each. Do we have to choose between them? Could they all be right? Could they all be wrong?

The following observations may help the reader to reach a conclusion.

First, it seems obvious that no one key unlocks the whole book. Each 'school' has seen some truths, but none has released all. When only one approach is used there is always some manipulation of the text.

Second, there is no reason why more than one may not be used. Texts have different meanings and applications. But some control is needed to avoid the arbitrary use of different approaches to bolster an opinion already decided upon before studying the scripture. This restraint is provided by the context and by constantly asking the question: was this the meaning intended by the divine author and the human writer?

Third, parts of each of the four methods can help understanding. Some elements from all four are compatible and can be used in conjunction with each other, though it must be added that other elements are quite incompatible and cannot be combined.

Fourth, the emphasis may change in different sections of the book. At each stage, the most appropriate method or methods of interpretation must be chosen and used. In the remainder of this chapter we shall illustrate this in practical terms by considering the three major divisions of the book:

THE BEGINNING (CHAPTERS 1–3)

This section is not very controversial, so is more frequently and confidently expounded than the rest (see, for example, *What Christ thinks of the Church* by John Stott, Lutterworth Press, 1958). Most are comfortable with the traditional interpretation (though uncomfortable with the application!). The problem with this section is that we *do* understand it, only too well. There are a few problems with details (the angels) and symbols (white stones and hidden manna). But the letters to the seven churches in Asia are not unlike other New Testament epistles. So which 'school' is appropriate?

The 'preterist' is surely right in directing our attention to the first century. Any true exegesis must *begin* with what this meant to them then. But need it end there?

The 'historicist' believes that the seven churches represent the whole church in *time*, seven consecutive epochs in church history. Ephesus covers the early church, Smyrna the Roman persecutions, Pergamum the time of Constantine, Thyatira the Middle Ages, Sardis the Reformation, Philadelphia the worldwide missionary movement and Laodicea the twentieth century. But the parallels are forced (Western churches may look 'Laodicean', but the Third-World ones are anything but!). This scheme simply doesn't fit.

The 'futurist' is even more bizarre, believing that the seven churches will be re-established in the very same cities of Asia just before Jesus returns, based on the mistaken assumption that 'I will come' (2:5, 16; 3:4) refers to the Second Advent. Actually, these churches have long since disappeared, their 'lampstands removed'.

The 'idealist' usually shares the 'preterist' view of this section, but adds the belief that the seven historical churches represent the whole Church in *space*. Ephesus represents the orthodox but loveless fellowships, Smyrna the suffering, Pergamum the enduring, Thyatira the corrupt, Sardis the dead, Philadelphia the feeble but evangelistic, Laodicea the lukewarm.

Whether they cover the entire range of church character between them is debatable. But the comfort and challenge of their example can be applied anywhere and any time.

So the preterist with a dash of idealist seems the right mixture for the first section.

THE MIDDLE (CHAPTERS 4–18)

This is where the differences are most acute. The opening vision of God's throne presents few problems and has inspired worship through the ages. It is when Jesus the Lion/Lamb releases disasters on the world and suffering on the church that the debate begins. When does this happen? It must be some-time between the second century (which was 'hereafter' to the seven churches; 4:1) and the Second Coming (in chapter 19).

The 'preterist' limits this section to the 'decline and fall of the Roman Empire'. But the fact remains that most predicted events, particularly the 'natural' catastrophes, simply did not happen during that period. Much of the text has to be treated as 'poetic licence', rather vaguely hinting at what might happen.

The 'historicist' has much the same problem when attempting to fit the whole of church history into these chapters, either as one continuous narrative or in repeated 'recapitulations'. The details will not fit.

The 'futurist' is, of course, free to believe in the literal fulfilment of the detailed forecast, since none of it has happened yet. Two features seem to confirm that this is nearer the correct application. First, the 'troubles' are clearly worse than anything the world has yet seen (as Jesus predicted in Matthew 24:21). Second, they seem to lead directly into the events at the end of history. But is that all? Has this section no relevance before then?

The 'idealist' is wrong to 'demythologize' this section, divorcing it from time altogether. But it is right to look for a message that can apply to any phase of church history. The clue lies in Scripture itself, which clearly teaches that future events cast their shadows ahead in time. Jesus is 'foreshadowed' in many ways in the Old Testament (as the letter to the Hebrews explains). The coming antichrist is preceded by 'many antichrists' (1 John 2:18); the coming false prophet by many false prophets (Matthew 24:11). The coming universal persecution is already experienced in many local regions. The 'Great Tribulation' is only different in scale from the 'much tribulation' which is normal at all times (John 16:33; Acts 14:22). So these chapters can help us to understand current trends as well as their ultimate climax.

So the futurist and a measure of idealist open up this section in the best way.

THE END (CHAPTERS 19–22)

Revelation seems to get clearer towards the end, but there are still some areas of controversy. Most take these chapters to refer to the ultimate future, the very 'last things' to happen, beginning with the return of Christ (in chapter 19).

The 'preterist' drops out here. Very few attempt to fit these chapters into the days of the early Church.

The 'historicist' school divides sharply in two. The 'linear' variety invariably see this section as the 'end-times', following the 'church age'. But the 'cyclical' find 'recapitulations' even here. Some see the Millennium in chapter 20 as a description of the church before the Second Coming in chapter 19! Others see the 'New Jerusalem' in chapter 21 as a description of the Millennium before the final judgement in chapter 20! Such radical dislocation of events are not justified by the text itself and suggest manipulation in the interests of theological systems and dogma.

The 'futurist' has few opponents in this section. The Second Coming, the Day of Judgement, and the new heaven and earth have clearly not yet arrived.

The 'idealist' has few proponents in this section. These tend to overlook the new earth altogether and talk about 'heaven' as the timeless sphere into which believers are transferred at death. The 'New Jerusalem' pictures this eternal realm (the 'heavenly Zion' of Hebrews 12:22), which is never expected to come 'down out of heaven' (in spite of Revelation 21:2, 10!).

So the futurist can be given a monopoly in handling this section.

In a later chapter we shall be sharing an 'introduction' to the text of Revelation itself, using the tools we have considered appropriate (which do not include the historicist). However, before we do that, there is one other important matter to consider.

The four 'schools' of interpretation share one common assumption: that the most important question is – WHEN? That is, when are the predictions fulfilled in time?

This is to start with the supposition that Revelation is primarily concerned with forecasting the future, to satisfy our curiosity or reduce our anxiety by revealing what is going to happen, both in the immediate and ultimate future.

But this is highly questionable. The New Testament never indulges in idle speculation, even warns against it. Every 'unveiling' of what lies ahead has a practical, indeed a moral purpose. The future is only revealed so that the present may be influenced by it.

So the fundamental question is not 'when'? but WHY? Why was Revelation written? Why was it revealed to John? Why was he told to pass it on? Why do we need to read and 'keep' these words?

Not just to tell us what is going to happen but to get us *ready* for what is going to happen. How do we arrive at that answer?

Sense of purpose

Why was the Book of Revelation written? The answer is readily accessible by asking another question: For whom was it written?

It was never intended to be a university textbook for theological staff or students. It is often they who have made it appear so complex that simple folk have been intimidated. Let one of them confess this:

> *We boldly affirm that the study of this book would present absolutely no possibility of error if the inconceivable, often ridiculous, prejudice of theologians in all ages had not so trammelled it and made it bristle with difficulties, that most readers shrink from it in alarm. Apart from these preconceptions, the Revelation would be the most simple, most transparent book that prophet ever penned* (Reuss, *in 1884, quoted in* The Prophecy Handbook, *World Bible Publishers, 1991*).

The situation has hardly improved since then, as a recent comment reveals:

> *It is one of the misfortunes of our expertise-oriented culture that when anything seems difficult it is sent off to the university to be figured out (Eugene Peterson, writing on Revelation in* Reversed Thunder, *HarperCollins, 1988, p. 200).*

This has led to a widespread notion that this book will not be understood by the 'layman' (whether that label is used in its ecclesiastical or educational sense).

Ordinary readers

It cannot be too strongly emphasized that Revelation was written for very ordinary people. It was addressed to the members of seven churches at a time when 'not many were wise by human standards; not many were influential; not many were of noble birth' (1 Corinthians 1:26).

It was said of Jesus that 'the common people heard him gladly' (Mark 12:37, Authorized Version). This was a tribute to them as well as to him. They recognized that he 'spoke with authority', that he knew what he was talking about. It is much easier to fool the highly educated!

The Book of Revelation yields its treasures to those who read it with a simple faith, an open mind and a tender heart.

A story has circulated in America which highlights the point, though it sounds like an apocryphal preacher's tale (as the pastor's little boy said: 'Daddy, was that story true, or was you just preaching?')! Apparently some theological students were tired and confused by lectures on 'apocalyptic' so decided to have a game of basketball in the campus gymnasium. While playing, they noticed the black janitor reading his Bible while waiting to lock up. They asked which part he was studying and were surprised to find he was going through Revelation. 'You don't understand that, do you?'

'Sure do.'

'What's it about, then?'

With eyes lit up and a broad smile came the reply: 'Simple! Jesus wins!!'

Of course, there's more to be said than that. But it's not a bad summary of the message. Plenty have studied the contents and missed the message. Common sense is a basic requirement. No one takes the whole book literally. No one takes it all symbolically. But where is the line to be drawn between the literal and the symbolical? This will have a profound effect on interpretation. Common sense will be a great help. The four horsemen are symbols, but the wars, bloodshed, famine and disease they represent clearly literal. The 'lake of fire' is a symbol of hell, but the unending 'torment' in it is literal (Revelation 20:10).

The rules of common speech may be usefully employed. Words should be taken in their plainest, simplest sense, unless clearly indicated otherwise. It should be assumed that speakers (including Jesus) and writers (including John) mean what they say. Their communications should be taken at face value.

Another such rule is that the same word in the same context is presumed to have the same meaning, again unless clearly indicated otherwise. To change the meaning of a word suddenly and without warning would be as confusing as changing the pronunciation or spelling. This rule directly affects the two 'resurrections' in Revelation 20.

Having said all this, we must add the necessary qualification that Revelation was written for ordinary folk in a very different time and place from ours. It is not surprising if some things obvious to them are obscure to us 2,000 years later and a similar number of miles away.

They were Gentiles of mixed race who lived in a Roman province, spoke Greek, read Jewish scriptures and were held together by a shared Christian faith. So we need to use as much knowledge of their background, culture and language as we can. The object of the exercise is to discover what *they* would have understood when they heard Revelation read aloud to them, perhaps at one sitting. That could be quite different from what we perceive as we read it silently, a short portion each day.

But the book is clearly for us in our day as well, or it would not be in the New Testament. The Lord must have intended this when he gave it to John. So we can assume that our distance in time and space is not an insuperable handicap.

A much more important factor than the cultural gap is the difference of circumstances. It is vital to ask what situation required the writing of this book. This is the master key required to unlock the whole volume. Behind every other book in the New Testament there is a reason for its being written, a need which it is designed to meet. Revelation is no exception.

Practical reasons

We have already said that its primary purpose was not to reveal a schedule of future events but to prepare people for what would happen. So what is coming for which, without this book, they would not be ready? The answer comes on the first page (1:9–10).

John, the writer, is already suffering for his faith. He is in prison, but not for any crime. He is a 'political' prisoner on the island of Patmos in the Aegean Sea (the modern equivalent would be Alcatraz or Robben Island). He has been arrested and exiled for religious reasons. His exclusive devotion to 'the word of God and the testimony of Jesus' is seen as treason by the authorities, a threat to the *pax Romana* based on polytheistic tolerance and an imperial cult. Citizens were expected to believe in many gods and the Emperor was one of them.

Towards the end of the first century, this situation came to a head, creating a crisis of conscience for Christians. Julius Caesar had been the first to proclaim himself divine. His successor, Augustus, had encouraged the building of temples in his honour; a number of these had been erected in Asia (now western Turkey). While Nero had begun the persecution of Christians (daubing them with pitch and burning them alive as torches for his nightly garden parties or sewing them in the skins of wild animals to be hunted by dogs), this was limited in duration and location.

It was the advent of Domitian in the last decade of the first century that inaugurated the fiercest attacks on Christians which would continue intermittently for 200 years. He demanded universal worship of himself, on pain of death. Once a year incense had to be thrown on an altar fire before his bust with an acclamation: 'Caesar is Lord.' The appointed day on which this had to be done was designated 'the Lord's Day'.

This was the very day on which Revelation began to be written. Modern readers may be forgiven for thinking it was a Sunday. Actually, it could have been, but Sunday was called 'the first day of the week' in the early church. Two elements in the Greek text indicate the annual imperial festival. One is the definite article (on '*the* Lord's day' not 'a Lord's day'). The other is the fact that 'Lord' is in the form of an adjective, not a noun ('the Lordy or Lordly day'), the very name given to it by Domitian, who also claimed the title: 'Lord and our God'.

Tough times lay ahead. For those who refused to say anything but 'Jesus is Lord', it would be a matter of life and death. The word 'witness' (in Greek: *martur*) would take on a new, deadly meaning. The church was facing its fiercest test so far. How many would remain loyal under such pressure?

After all, John was the only one of the 12 apostles left. All the others had already suffered a martyr's death. Christian tradition records that Andrew died on an X-shaped cross in Patras of Achaia, Bartholomew (Nathaniel) was flayed alive in Armenia, James (brother of John) was beheaded by Herod Agrippa in Jerusalem, James (son of Cleopas and Mary) was thrown from the pinnacle of the temple and stoned, Jude (Thaddeus) was shot with arrows in Armenia, Matthew was slain by the sword in Parthia, Peter was crucified upside down in Rome, Philip was hanged on a pillar in Hieropolis in Phrygia, Simon (Zelotes) was crucified in Persia, Thomas was slain with a spear in India, Matthias was stoned and beheaded. Paul also had been beheaded in Rome. So the writer of Revelation was only too aware of the cost of loyalty to Jesus. He did not then know that he would be the only apostle to die a natural death.

Revelation is a 'manual for martyrdom'. It calls believers to 'be faithful, even to the point of death' (2:10). Martyrs figure largely in its pages.

Believers are encouraged to 'stick it out'. One frequent exhortation is to 'endure', a passive attitude. Right in the middle of the biggest trouble comes the plea: 'This calls for patient endurance on the part of the saints who obey God's commandments and remain faithful to Jesus' (14:12). This may be said to be the key verse in the whole book.

But there is also a call to an active attitude in suffering for Jesus: to 'overcome'. This verb is used even more frequently than 'endure' and may be said to be the key word in the whole book.

Each letter to the seven churches concludes with a call to each member to be an 'overcomer', that is, to overcome all temptations and pressures, both inside and outside the church. To lapse from truly Christian belief and behaviour is to be unfaithful to Jesus.

The message is not just that Christ wins, but that Christians must also win through. They are to follow the Lord who said: 'Take heart! I have overcome the world' (John 16:33) and who now says in Revelation: 'You also must overcome the world.'

Of course, that is why this book becomes so much more meaningful to Christians under persecution. Maybe this is also why Western Christians in comfortable churches fail to find it relevant. It has to be read through tears.

The book offers two incentives to encourage the persecuted to 'overcome'. One is positive: *reward*. Many prizes are offered to those who persevere – the right to eat of the tree of life in the paradise of God; never to be hurt by the second death; to eat the hidden manna and be given a white stone with a secret new name on it; to have authority to rule the nations; to sit with Jesus on his throne; to be dressed in white and made a pillar in the temple of God bearing his name and never to leave it. Above all, and beyond all the suffering, the overcoming believer is promised a place in the new heaven and earth, enjoying God's presence for ever and ever. The prospect is glorious.

But there is a negative motivation as well: *punishment*. What is the fate of believers who are unfaithful under pressure? In a word, they will have none of the above blessings. Worse than that, they will share the fate of unbelievers in the 'lake of fire'. Two verses alone, taken from first and last sections, confirm this awful possibility.

'He who overcomes … I will never erase his name from the book of life' (3:5). If language means anything at all, it means that those who do not overcome are in danger of having their names erased (literally, 'scraped off' the parchment with a knife). The 'book of life' appears in four books of the Bible (Exodus 32:32; Psalm 69:28; Philippians 4:3; Revelation 3:5).

Three of these contexts mention names of the people of God being blotted out after they have sinned against the Lord. To read the verse in Revelation as if it could include 'he who doesn't overcome' in the promise as well is to make the reward meaningless.

'He who overcomes will inherit all this [the new heaven and earth, with the New Jerusalem] and I will be his God and he will be my son. But the cowardly, the faithless, the immoral … their place will be in the fiery lake of burning sulphur. This is the second death' (21:7–8). It needs to be remembered that the whole of Revelation is directed to believers, not unbelievers. Throughout, it is addressed to 'the saints' and 'his servants'. The reference here is to cowardly and faithless believers. This is confirmed by the word 'but', directly contrasting those deserving such a fate with the believers who 'overcome'.

In other words, Revelation sets two destinies before *Christians*. They will either be raised with Christ and share his reign, ending up in the new universe. Or they will lose their inheritance in the Kingdom and end up in hell.

This alternative is confirmed elsewhere in the New Testament. The Gospel of Matthew is a 'manual for discipleship' containing five major discourses addressed to 'sons of the Kingdom'. Yet most of Jesus' teaching on hell is to be found here and all but two of his warnings are addressed to his disciples. The Sermon on the Mount (in chapters 5–7), which blesses those who are persecuted because of Jesus, goes on to speak of hell and concludes with a reminder that there are two destinies. The missionary commissioning (in chapter 10) includes the charge: 'Do not be afraid of those who kill the body but cannot kill the soul. Rather be afraid of the one who can destroy both body and soul in hell' (verse 28) and 'whoever disowns me before men, I will disown him before my Father in heaven' (verse 33). The Olivet discourse (in chapters

24–25) condemns slothful and careless servants of the master to being 'assigned a place with the hypocrites' (24:51) and 'thrown outside into the darkness, where there will be weeping and gnashing of teeth' (25:30).

Paul takes the same line when reminding Timothy of a 'trustworthy saying':

> If we died with him,
>   we will also live with him;
> If we endure,
>   we will also reign with him.
> If we disown him,
>   He will also disown us ... (2 Timothy 2:11–12)

Many Christians deny the implications of all this. Certainly there is more to be said (the author has dealt more fully with this vital question in a volume entitled *Once Saved, Always Saved?* Hodder & Stoughton, 1996). Meanwhile, the position in Revelation seems very clear. It is even possible for believers to lose their 'share in the tree of life and in the holy city' simply by tampering with the text of the book (22:19), thus changing its message.

We could summarize the aim of Revelation by saying it was written to exhort Christians facing immense pressures to 'endure' and 'overcome' and thus avoid the 'second death' by keeping their names in the 'book of life'. We shall find that every chapter and verse fits easily into this overall purpose, as we look at the shape or structure of the whole book.

The structure of Revelation

If we have been right in defining the purpose of Revelation as the preparation of believers to face persecution and even martyrdom, it should be possible to relate this to every part of the book. Moreover, the overall structure should reveal a development of this theme.

We shall construct a number of outlines by analysing the contents from different perspectives and for different purposes, starting with the simplest. The most obvious division occurs at 4:1, with the radical shift in viewpoint from earth to heaven and from the present situation to the future prospects:

1–3   Present
4–22   Future

The larger second part also divides neatly between the bad news and the good news. The change from one to the other comes in 19. So now we have:

1–3   Present
4–22   Future
         4–18   *Bad news*
         20–22   *Good news*

Now we consider how each section relates to the main purpose of the book. That is, how does each section prepare believers for the coming 'Big Trouble'? We can expand the outline thus:

1–3   Present
         Things must be put right now.
4–22   Future

4–18   *Bad news:* things will get much worse
        before they get better.

20–22   *Good news:* things will get much better after
        they get worse.

Only one more item remains to be added, namely, chapter 19.
What occurs in this chapter to change the whole situation? The
Second Coming of Jesus to planet earth! This is really the framework of the whole book, according to the prologue and epilogue
(1:7 and 22:20). We can now insert '19 Jesus returns' between the
bad and good news (rather than repeat the outline unnecessarily,
readers are invited to write it themselves in the gap left above).

If this simple outline is kept in mind when reading through
the book, many things will become clearer. Above all, the unity
of the whole book will become apparent. Its objective is
achieved in three phases.

First, Jesus tells the churches that they must deal with
internal problems if they are to face external pressures. Compromise in belief or behaviour, tolerance of idolatry or immorality, weaken the church from within.

Second, Jesus, who was always noted for his honesty, shows
them the worst that can happen to them. They will never have
to go through anything worse! And the very worst time ahead
will be at most only a few years.

Third, Jesus reveals the wonders that will follow. To throw
away such eternal prospects for the sake of avoiding temporary
troubles would be the greatest tragedy of all.

In all three ways, Jesus is encouraging his followers to
'endure' and 'overcome' until he gets back. One verse sums it
all up: 'Only hold on to what you have until I come' (2:25).
Then he can say: 'Come and share your master's happiness'
(Matthew 25:21).

Of course, there are other ways of analysing the book. A 'topical' outline is more like an index of subjects and will assist us to 'find our way around' the book.

Such an outline will ignore the switch from earth to heaven and back again. We can work with three periods of time:

A. What is already happening in the present (1–5).
B. What will happen in the nearer future (6–19).
C. What will happen in the distant future (20–22).

We will then note the main features of each period and seek to list these in a way that can easily be memorized. Here is one example of such a 'catalogue' of events:

A. The present
    1–3   One ascended Lord
             Seven assorted lampstands
    4–5   Creator and creatures
             Lion and Lamb
B. The near future
    6–16   Seals, trumpets, bowls
             Devil, antichrist, false prophet
    17–19   Babylon – last capital
             Armageddon – last battle
C. The far future
    20   Millennial reign
             Judgement Day
    21–22   New heaven and earth
             New Jerusalem

Note that chapters 4–5 are now in the first division. That is because the 'action' leading to the 'Big Trouble' actually begins with chapter 6. Chapter 19 is now in the second division because the 'Big Trouble' ends here, with Christ defeating the 'unholy trinity'.

This kind of outline is easily memorized and provides a useful 'ready reference' when looking up particular subjects.

It is important to do this kind of exercise before getting down to a closer look at the several sections. There is an over-used proverb about 'not being able to see the wood for the trees'! Revelation is one of the easiest books in which to get so interested in the details that the overall thrust is lost sight of.

However, it is now time to exchange the telescope for a microscope – or at least for a magnifying glass!

The contents of Revelation

In a book this size it is impossible to include a full commentary. What we intend to do is give an introduction to each section that will enable the Bible student to 'read, mark, learn and in-wardly digest the same', as the Book of Common Prayer puts it.

We shall highlight the major features, tackle some of the problems and generally help the reader to keep on course through some of the hazards. Many questions will have to be left unanswered, but these can be followed up in some of the published commentaries (George Eldon Ladd's is one of the best; Eerdmans, 1972).

The suggestion is that each part of Revelation is read before and after the relevant section in this chapter.

Chapters 1–3: The Church on Earth

This is by far the most straightforward, easy to read and under-stand. It is like paddling at the edge of the sea, after which you may find yourself out of your depth and in the grip of an undertow, swirling around in a panic!

Though frequently describing itself as a 'prophecy', Revelation is actually in the form of a letter (compare 1:4–6 with the opening 'address' of other epistles). However, it is sent to seven churches rather than one. While containing a particular message for each, it is clearly intended that all should hear each other's.

After the usual Christian greeting ('grace and peace'), the main theme is announced: 'he is coming', an event which will cause unhappiness to the world but joy to the Church. This event is absolutely certain ('Amen').

The 'sender' of the letter is God himself, the Lord of time, who is, was and is to come, the Alpha and Omega (the first and the last letters of the Greek alphabet, symbolizing the beginning and end of everything). The same titles will be given to Jesus, by himself (1:17; 22:13), proof that he believed in his own deity.

The 'secretary' who writes the letter down is the apostle John, exiled to the eight-miles-by-four island of Patmos in the Dodecanese of the Aegean Sea, a political prisoner for religious reasons.

The contents were given in verbal and visual form. Note that he 'heard' something before he 'saw' anything. The voice commanding him to write was followed by an overwhelming vision of Jesus as John had never seen him before: snow-white hair, blazing eyes, thundering voice, sharp tongue, glowing feet. Even on the Mount of Transfiguration, he had never looked like this. No wonder John swooned, until he heard some very familiar words: 'Don't be afraid'.

Every other great figure of history was alive and is dead. Jesus alone was dead and is alive, 'for ever and ever' (1:18; literally 'to the ages of the ages').

John is told to write 'what is now' (chapters 1–3) and 'what will take place later' (chapters 4–22). The word for the present is the state of the seven churches of Asia, each of which has a 'guardian angel' and for which Jesus has oversight (as well as insight and foresight!). They were represented in the original vision by seven stars (the angels) and seven lampstands (the churches). Note that Jesus characteristically 'walks' around them, as John must have done when he was free. In the Gospels, most of Jesus' messages were delivered and miracles were done as he walked 'in the way', both before his death and after his resurrection.

The seven letters to the seven churches are best studied together and compared with each other. It is very illuminating when they are written out side by side, which emphasizes both their similarities and differences.

It becomes immediately obvious that their form is identical, comprising seven elements (yet another 'seven'):

1. Address:
   'To the angel of the church in …'
2. Attribute:
   'These are the words of him who …'
3. Approval:
   'I know your deeds …'
4. Accusation:
   'Yet I hold this against you'
5. Advice:
   '… or else I will come and …'
6. Assurance:
   'To him who overcomes, I will …'
7. Appeal:
   '… let him hear what the Spirit says …'

The only variation from this order is in the last four letters, where the final two items are reversed (the reason for this is not apparent). We shall now compare and contrast the letters.

THE ADDRESS

This is exactly the same in all seven, except for the named destination. The cities are on a circular route, starting in the major port of Ephesus (a church of which we have more information than any other of those days), heading north up the coast, then inland to the east and finally south to the rich valley of the river Meander.

The only point of debate is whether the word *angelos* (literally 'messenger') refers to a heavenly or human person. Since everywhere else in Revelation it is rightly translated as 'angel', the strong presumption is that it is the same here. Angels are very much involved with churches (even noting hairstyles of worshippers! 1 Corinthians 11:10). Since John is totally isolated, heavenly 'messengers' would have to deliver the letters. It is only modern scepticism about the existence of angels that has led to the translation: 'minister' (presumably with the title 'Rev.'!).

THE ATTRIBUTE

It is noticeable that Jesus never refers to himself by name, only by titles, many of them quite new. In fact, he has over 250 titles, the largest number of any historical personage (it is a useful devotional exercise to list them). In each letter, the title of Jesus is carefully chosen to describe an aspect of his character which that church has tended to forget or needs to consider. Some are to be found in John's original vision of him. All are very significant. The 'key of David' points to his fulfilment of the messianic hopes of Israel. 'Ruler of God's creation' signifies his universal authority (Matthew 28:18).

THE APPROVAL

This opens the most intimate part of each letter, switching from the third person ('him') to the first ('I'). Is this the same

person? The 'him' certainly refers to Christ, but the 'I' could
be the Spirit, the 'Spirit of Christ', of course. Later comments
(e.g. 'I have received authority from my Father' in 2:27) favour
the former.

'I know' is a claim to be totally aware, both of their internal
state and external situation. His knowledge, and therefore his
understanding, is total. His judgement is accurate, his opinion
crucial and his honesty transparent.

Above all, he knows their 'works', that is, their deeds, their
actions. This emphasis on works runs right through Revelation.
That is because its theme is judgement. Jesus is coming again
– to judge the living and the dead. We are justified by faith,
but we shall be judged by works (2 Corinthians 5:10). Jesus
approves good works and encourages their continuance.

When the letters are viewed side by side, it is immediately
apparent that Jesus has nothing good to say about two of them,
Sardis and Laodicea. Yet these are both 'successful' to human
eyes. Jesus' opinion may be very different from ours. Large
congregations, big collections and full programmes are not
necessarily signs of spiritual health.

Five of the churches are commended: Ephesus for effort,
patience, persistence and discernment (rejecting false apostles);
Smyrna for its courage in the face of opposition and depriva-
tion (though adjacent to a 'synagogue of Satan', possibly an
occult form of Judaism); Pergamum for not denying the faith
under pressure, even when one member was martyred (though
under the shadow of the 'throne of Satan', a gigantic temple
now re-erected in an East Berlin museum); Thyatira for its
love, faith, patience and progress; Philadelphia for its costly
fidelity (with another 'synagogue of Satan' nearby).

In passing we note that Jesus frequently speaks of Satan,
who is behind all hostility towards the churches. He is also
responsible for the looming crisis they will face, 'the hour of

trial that is going to come upon the whole world to test those who live on the earth' (3:10).

Finally, how characteristic of Jesus to commend before he criticizes, an example followed by the apostles. Paul thanked God that the Corinthians had all the 'spiritual gifts' (1 Corinthians 1:4–7) before he corrected their abuse of them. Of course, he also encountered church situations where this was not possible, as in Galatia. But the principle is one to be emulated by all Christians.

THE ACCUSATION

Again, two are exempt from criticism, Smyrna and Philadelphia. What a relief they must have felt when their letters were read out! They are weaker than the others and already suffering, but they have remained faithful, which pleases Jesus more than anything else (Matthew 25:21, 23).

What was wrong with the others? Ephesus had forsaken its 'first love' (for the Lord, each other or lost sinners? Probably all three, since they are interconnected); Pergamum was into idolatry and immorality (syncretism and permissiveness are the modern counterparts); Thyatira was guilty of the same things (as a result of listening to 'Jezebel', a false prophetess); Sardis was for ever starting new ventures, giving it the reputation of being a 'live' church, but they were not kept up or seen through to the finish (does that strike a chord?); Laodicea was sick, but didn't know it.

This last letter is perhaps the best known and most striking. They prided themselves on being a warm fellowship, with a warm welcome for the many visitors. But 'lukewarm' churches make Jesus feel sick. He can handle icy-cold or piping-hot ones more easily! This is a reference to the salty hot springs covering a hillside outside the city (the 'white castle' of Pamukkale is still a popular 'spa' for health seekers); by the time the stream reached Laodicea it was 'lukewarm' and acted as an emetic, causing its drinkers to vomit.

Jesus has stopped attending services here! He cannot be found inside – but stands just outside. Verse 20 is probably the most abused text in Scripture and has been almost universally used as an evangelistic invitation and in counselling enquirers. It has nothing to do with becoming a Christian. Indeed, it gives quite a wrong impression when used in this way (actually, it is the sinner who is on the outside needing to knock and enter the Kingdom, of which Jesus is the door; Luke 11:5–10; John 3:5; 10:7). The 'door' in 3:20 is the church door in Laodicea. The verse is a prophetic message to a church which has lost Christ and it is full of hope. It only takes one member who wants to sit at his table with him to get Christ back inside! For a fuller treatment of this verse and the New Testament way to become a Christian, see my book *The Normal Christian Birth* (Hodder and Stoughton, 1989).

Before we leave this section, it needs to be pointed out that these accusations stem from the love of Jesus for the churches. He says this himself: 'as many as I love I reprove and chasten' (3:19). In fact, the absence of such discipline could be a sign of not belonging to his family at all (Hebrews 12:7–8)!

He is not wanting to put them down, but lift them up. Above all, he seeks to get them ready for pending pressure, which will 'test' them (3:10). If they compromise now, they will surrender then. That could cost them their inheritance.

THE ADVICE

There is a word of counsel for all seven churches. Even the two of which he thoroughly approves are exhorted to keep up the good work, to 'hold on to what you have until I come' (2:25).

The other five are cautioned with two words: 'remember' and 'repent'. They are to call to mind what they once were and what they ought to be. And true repentance involves much more than regret or remorse; it requires confession and correction.

He warns those that spurn his appeal that he 'will come' and deal with them. There will be a time when it will be too late to put things right. Sometimes this refers to his Second Coming, when the 'crown of life' will be given to those who have been 'faithful, even to the point of death' (2:10; compare 2 Timothy 4:6–8), but those who are not ready will hear the dreadful words: 'I don't know you' (Matthew 25:12).

Usually, 'I will come' refers to an earlier 'visitation' to a single church, to remove its 'lampstand' (2:5). Jesus has a ministry of closing churches down! A compromised church that is not willing to be corrected is worse than useless to the Kingdom of God. It is better to remove such a poor advertisement for the gospel altogether.

We could summarize this part of the letters: 'put it right, keep it up or I will close it down'.

THE ASSURANCE

It is noticeable that the call to 'overcome' is not addressed to a church as a whole, but to each individual member. Judgement is always individual, whether for the purpose of reward or punishment, never corporate (note 'each one' in 2 Corinthians 5:10). There is no suggestion of leaving a corrupt church and catching a chariot to a better one down the road! Neither is a person excused compromise because their whole church is slipping. The wrong trends in a fellowship are not to be followed. In other words, a Christian may have to learn to resist pressures in the church first before facing them in the world. If we cannot 'overcome' the former, we are unlikely to 'overcome' the latter.

Jesus has no hesitation in offering rewards as incentives (5:12). He himself endured the cross, scorning its shame, 'for the joy set before him' (Hebrews 12:2). In each of the letters he encourages 'overcomers' to think of the prizes awaiting those who 'press on toward the goal' (Philippians 3:14).

Just as his title in each letter is taken from the first chapter, the rewards he offers are taken from the last chapters. They will come in the ultimate future rather than the immediate present. Only those who have faith that he keeps his promises will be motivated by distant compensations.

Once again, we must realize that the joys of the new heaven and earth are not for all believers, but only for those who overcome the pressures of temptation and persecution (21:7–8 makes this abundantly clear). It is those who remain obedient and faithful 'to the end' (2:26) who will be saved (compare Matthew 10:22; 24:13; Mark 13:13; Luke 21:19).

THE APPEAL

The final call, 'he that has an ear, let him hear', is a familiar conclusion to Jesus' words (Matthew 13:9, for example). Its meaning becomes clear in the light of one of the most frequently quoted texts from the Old Testament in the New: 'You will be ever hearing, but never understanding ... they hardly hear with their ears ... otherwise they might ... hear with their ears, understand with their hearts and turn, and I would heal them' (Isaiah 6:9–10, quoted in Matthew 13:13–15; Mark 4:12; Luke 8:10; Acts 28:26–27).

Jesus knew that this would be the general response from the Jews. Now he is challenging Christians not to have the same reaction. He is highlighting the difference between hearing and heeding a message. It is a question of how much notice is taken of what he says. His words in Revelation will only be a blessing if they are read and 'kept', that is, not just taken into the ear but 'taken to heart' (1:3). A parent whose child has ignored the order to 'put that down' will say, 'Did you hear what I said?', knowing full well that it was heard, but was not heeded.

Quite simply, the closing remark in each of the letters to the seven churches means that Jesus expects a reply, in the form of a positive response of obedience. He has the right to expect this. He is Lord.

Chapters 4–5: God in Heaven

This section is relatively straightforward and needs little introduction. In particular, chapter 4 is probably familiar in the context of worship; it is often read to stimulate praise and has provided the content for many hymns and choruses. It gives a glimpse of that heavenly adoration of which all earthly worship is an echo.

John has been invited to 'come up here' (4:1) and see what heaven looks like, a privilege shared by few during their lifetime (Paul had a similar experience; 2 Corinthians 12:1–6). It is the place where God reigns and from which he rules. 'Throne' is the keyword and it occurs 16 times. Notice the emphasis on 'sitting' (4:2, 9, 10; 5:1). This is the control centre of the 'Kingdom of Heaven'.

The scene is breathtakingly beautiful, almost defying description. Green rainbows (!), golden crowns, thunder and lightning, blazing lamps – one can almost imagine John's eyes darting from one striking feature to another as he gazes in awe and wonder. In trying to describe what he can see of God himself, he can only compare this with two of the most brilliant gemstones he has ever seen before (jasper and carnelian).

Above all, there is a peaceful aspect to the whole scene, expressed as a 'sea of glass', stretching to the horizon. The sharp contrast with profound disturbances on earth (from chapter 6 onwards) is clearly intentional. God reigns supreme above all the battles between good and evil. He does not have to struggle; even Satan has to ask his permission before he can touch a human being (Job 1). He is not even surprised by anything. He knows exactly how to deal with whatever arises, since that also can only be what he allows.

He is God, not man. He is therefore worthy of worship (the word derives from 'worth-ship', telling someone how much they are worth to you). The Creator receives non-stop praise from the creatures he has made. The four 'living' ones are only 'like' a lion, ox, man and eagle; together they may represent all creatures from the four corners of the earth (though there are 20 other interpretations!). Their praise is vaguely 'trinitarian': 'holy' three times and God in three dimensions of time – past, present and future.

Twenty-four elders comprise the 'council' of heaven (Jeremiah 23:18). Almost certainly they represent the two covenant peoples of God, Israel and the Church (notice the 24 names on the New Jerusalem's gates and foundations; 21:12–14). They have 'crowns' and 'thrones', but only delegated authority.

There is no action in chapter 4, other than unceasing worship. It is a permanent scene with no time reference. With chapter 5 the action begins – with the search for someone 'in heaven and earth', someone 'worthy to break the seals and open the scroll'.

The significance of the scroll becomes apparent in the light of events. On it must be written the programme which will bring to an end the age of earthly history in which we live. Breaking its seals begins the countdown.

Until this happens, the world must continue in its present state. The 'present evil age' must be closed before the 'age to come' can open. There must be a decisive termination of the 'kingdoms of the world' if the 'Kingdom of God' is to be universally established on the earth. That is why John 'wept and wept' in frustration and grief when no one was found 'worthy' to set this in motion.

But why was this a problem? God himself had released many judgements on the earth through history. Why not the final ones? Either he does not choose to do so or does not feel he is qualified to do so! This last thought is not so bizarre or even blasphemous as some might think, in the light of what is said about the one Person who is found to be 'worthy'.

Who is it? Someone who is both a 'Lion' and a 'Lamb'! Actually, the contrast between the two is not as great as many assume. The Lamb is male and fully mature, as was every lamb used in sacrifice ('one year old'; Exodus 12:5). In this case, the 'Ram', as we should really say, has seven horns (one more than Jacob sheep), signifying perfect power and seven eyes, signifying perfect oversight. Yet it has been 'slain' as a sacrifice.

The lion is king of the jungle, but here of the tribe of Judah and rooted in the Davidic dynasty. So we have a unique combination of the sovereign Lion and the sacrificial Lamb, which corresponds to the coming king and suffering servant predicted by the Hebrew prophets (e.g. Isaiah 9–11 and 42–53).

But it is not just what he is, but what he has done, that fits him to release the troubles that will bring the world to an end, for 'end' can mean two things: termination and consummation. He will bring it to the latter.

He has prepared a people to take over the government of the world. He has purchased them, at the price of his own blood, out of every ethnic group in the human race. He has trained them in royal and priestly duties in God's service and thus prepared them for the responsibility of *reigning on the earth* (this is fully developed in Revelation 20:4–6).

Only someone who has done all this is able to begin the series of disasters that will bring all other regimes down. To destroy a bad system without having a good one ready to replace it can only lead to anarchy.

And he himself is a worthy sovereign over the government he has prepared, precisely because he was willing to give his all to make it possible. It was because he became 'obedient to death – even death on a cross!' that 'God exalted him to the highest place' (Philippians 2:8–9).

No wonder thousands of angels agree, in musical acclamation, that it is only right to give him power, wealth, wisdom, strength, honour, glory and praise. Then all the creatures in the universe join the choir's anthem, though with one significant addition. The power, honour, glory and praise should be shared between the one sitting on the throne and the one standing in the centre in front of him, the Father and the Son together. For it was a joint effort. They were both involved. They both suffered to make it all possible, though in very different ways.

Nothing reveals more clearly the divinity of our Lord Jesus Christ as the offering of unqualified praise and worship to both him and God together.

Chapters 6–16: Satan on Earth

This section is the heart of the book and the most difficult to understand and apply.

We are into the bad news. Things will get much worse before they get better. At least there is the comfort of knowing that the situation cannot ever be worse than that foretold in these chapters. But that's bad enough!

There are three major problems for interpreters.

First, what is the *order* of events? It is quite difficult to put them all on a time chart, as those who attempt this soon discover.

Second, what do all the *symbols* mean? Some are clear. Some are explained. But some are a problem (the 'pregnant woman' in chapter 12 is a case in point).

Third, when is the *fulfilment* of the predictions? In our past, our present or our future? Have they already happened, are they happening right now or are they yet to happen?

We shall concentrate on the order of events, which is far from clear at the first reading, looking at the symbols as we come to them. The task is complicated by the insertion of three features which are out of order, scattered seemingly at random through these chapters.

First, there are *digressions*. In the form of 'interludes' or parentheses, these deal with subjects that seem to be outside the main stream of events.

Second, there are *recapitulations*. From time to time the narrative seems to go back on its track, recalling events already mentioned.

Third, there are *anticipations*. Events are mentioned without explanation until later in the story (for example, 'Armageddon' first appears in 16:16, but does not happen until chapter 19).

These have led to misunderstanding and speculation, notably in the 'cyclical historicist' interpretation already discussed. We shall follow a simpler route, working from the obvious to the obscure.

Reading through these chapters at one sitting, the most striking features are the three sequences of seals, trumpets and bowls. The symbolism in these is comparatively easy to decode.

Seals: 1. White horse – military aggression
            2. Red horse – bloodshed
            3. Black horse – famine
            4. Green horse – disease, epidemics

                     * * *

            5. Persecution and prayer
            6. Tremor and terror

                     * * *

7. Silence in heaven, listening to prayers which are then answered in a final catastrophe: severe earthquake

Trumpets:
1. Scorched earth
2. Polluted sea
3. Contaminated water
4. Reduced sunlight

* * *

5. Insects and plague (five months)
6. Oriental invasion (200 million)

* * *

7. The Kingdom comes, the world is taken over by God and Christ after a severe earthquake

Bowls:
1. Boils on the skin
2. Blood in the sea
3. Blood from the springs
4. Burning by the sun

* * *

5. Darkness
6. Armageddon

* * *

7. Hailstorm and severe earthquake, leading to international collapse

As soon as they are laid out like this a number of things become clear:

The events are not totally unfamiliar. They are vaguely reminiscent of the plagues in Egypt when Moses confronted Pharaoh, even down to frogs and locusts (Exodus 7–11). They are also happening today on a local or regional scale. For example, the sequence of four horses can be observed in many parts of the world, each a result of the previous one. The major novelty is the universal scale on which they happen here, as if the troubles have spread worldwide.

Each series divides into three parts. The first four belong together, the most notable example being the 'four horsemen of the Apocalypse' as they have become known since the artist Albrecht Dürer portrayed them. The next two are not quite so closely related and the last one stands on its own. The last three in each are labelled 'woes', a word indicating curses.

Looking at the three series together, there appears to be an *intensification* in the severity of events. While a quarter of mankind perish in the 'seals', one third of the remainder fail to survive the 'trumpets'. Furthermore, there is a progression in the causes of disaster. The 'seals' are of human origin; the 'trumpets' seem to be a natural deterioration of the environment; the 'bowls' are directly poured out by angelic agents.

There is also an *acceleration* of events. The 'seals' seem quite spread out in time, but the later series appear to be measured in months or even days.

All this suggests a progression in the three series, which brings us to the question of the relation between them. The most obvious answer is that they are *successive*, which may be represented thus: Seals: 1234567, then trumpets: 1234567, then bowls: 1234567. In other words, the series simply follow each other.

But it is not quite as simple as this! A careful study reveals that the seventh in each case seems to refer to the same event (a severe earthquake on a world scale is the common factor; 8:5; 11:19; 16:18). This has led to an alternative theory, beloved by the 'cyclical historicist' school, which believes the series are *simultaneous*, thus:

Seals: 1 2 3 4 5 6 7
Trumpets: 1 2 3 4 5 6 7
Bowls: 1 2 3 4 5 6 7

In other words, they cover the same period (usually held to be the whole time between the First and Second Advents) from different angles.

A more convincing, but more complicated pattern combines these two insights, treating the first six as successive and the seventh as simultaneous:

Seals: 1 2 3 4 5 6   7
Trumpets: 1 2 3 4 5 6   7
Bowls: 1 2 3 4 5 6 7

In other words, each series advances on the previous one but all climax in the same catastrophic end. This seems to best fit the evidence and is mainly held by the 'futurist' school who believe all three series still lie ahead in history.

All three concentrate on what will happen to the world. In passing, the reaction of human beings should be noted. While recognizing that these terrible tragedies are evidence of the wrath of God (and the Lamb's!), the human response is one of terror (6:15–17) and curses on God (16:21) rather than repentance (9:20–21), even though the gospel of forgiveness is still available (14:6). It is a sad comment on the hardness of the human heart, but it is true to life. In disasters we either turn towards God or against him (the last words of crashing airline pilots often curse God; they are usually edited out of the 'black box' recording before it is played at the enquiry).

It is time to look at the chapters inserted between the three series of seals, trumpets and bowls – or rather, within them, as we shall see. There are three such insertions: chapter 7, chapters

10–11 and chapters 12–14. The first two sections are put between the sixth and seventh seals and trumpets, but the third is put before the first bowl, as if there is no time-scale for it between the sixth and seventh bowls. We can put this in diagram form, using the previous illustration:

Seals:	1 2 3 4 5 6 (ch. 7)		7
Trumpets:		1 2 3 4 5 6 (chs. 10–11)	7
Bowls:		(chs. 12–14) 1 2 3 4 5 6 7	

We now have a complete outline of chapters 6–16.

Whereas the three series of seals, trumpets and bowls are primarily concerned with what will happen to the *world*, the three insertions deal with what will happen to the *Church*. Here we are given information about God's people during this terrible upheaval. How will they be affected? Since Revelation aims to prepare the 'saints' for what is to come, these insertions are more relevant and important for them.

Chapters 7: the two groups

Between the sixth and seventh seals, we catch a glimpse of two distinct kinds of people in two very different places.

On the one hand, *a limited number of Jews are protected on earth* (verses 1–8). God has not rejected Israel (Romans 11:1, 11). He made an unconditional promise that they would survive as long as the universe lasted (Jeremiah 31:35–37). He will keep his word. They have a future.

The numbers seem somewhat arbitrary, even artificial. Perhaps they are 'round' numbers or maybe symbolic in some way. What is clear is that it will be a very limited proportion of a nation now numbered in millions. And the total will be equally divided between the 12 tribes, without favouring any. This means that the 10 tribes taken to Assyria were not 'lost' to

God and that he will preserve the survivors of each tribe that are known to him. There is one lost tribe, Dan, which rebelled against God's will for it and was replaced – in much the same way as Judas Iscariot among the 12 apostles. Both are warnings against taking our place in God's purposes for granted.

On the other hand, *an uncountable number of Christians are protected in heaven* (verses 8–17). The international crowd stand in an honoured place before the King, joining with the elders and living creatures in their songs of praise. But they add one new note of praise: for their 'salvation'.

John does not realize their significance and confesses ignorance of their qualifications for such honour. One of the elders enlightens him: 'These are they who are coming out of the Great Tribulation' (verse 14; the tense of the verb clearly indicates a continuing procession of individuals and groups through the whole time of trouble). How are they escaping? Not by one sudden and secret 'rapture', but by death, most by martyrdom, which figures so prominently in these very chapters (we have already heard the cries of their 'souls' for vengeance; 6:9–11).

But it is the shedding of the Lamb's blood rather than their own that has rescued them. It was his suffering, not theirs, a sacrifice that atoned for their sins and made them clean enough to stand in God's presence and offer their service.

But God is mindful of what they have suffered for his Son's sake and he will make sure that they will 'never again' experience such pain. The scorching sun will not burn them (16:8–9). They will be looked after by the 'good shepherd' (Psalm 23; John 10). They will be refreshed with water, 'living' (fizzy!) rather than 'still' (John 4:14; 7:38; Revelation 21:6; 21:1, 17). And God, like every parent with a weeping child, will 'wipe away every tear from their eyes' (21:4). Note that being in heaven now is a foretaste of life on the new earth.

Chapters 10–11: the two witnesses

Between the sixth and seventh trumpets, attention is focused on the human channels through which the divine revelations are communicated. The keyword in both chapters is 'prophesy' (10:11; 11:3, 6). At the beginning of the Church age, John in Patmos is the prophet; at the end there will be two 'witnesses' who will prophesy in the city of Jerusalem.

There is a sense of impending disaster in the spectacular appearance of two 'mighty' angels. The terrible truths uttered by the first in a thunderous voice are for John alone and must not be communicated to anyone else (compare 2 Corinthians 12:4). The second announces that there will be no more delay in the build-up of events – the seventh trumpet will be the climax (confirming our conclusion that the seventh seal, trumpet and bowl all refer to the same 'end').

The last and worst part of the 'bad news' is about to be given. It is on a 'little scroll' (an expanded, more detailed, version of part of the larger one already opened?). John is told to 'eat it' (we would say: 'digest it'). It will taste 'sweet and sour', sweet at first but sour when it begins to sink in (a reaction that many have to the whole Book of Revelation when they begin to grasp its message).

John is told to 'prophesy again', to continue his work of foretelling the future of the world. Then he is 'shown' around the city of Jerusalem and its temple. He measures its courts, but not the outermost one for Gentile worshippers, since they will be coming to 'trample' on the city rather than pray in it. They will, however, encounter two extraordinary persons who will preach to them about the God they despise.

The result will be death for preachers and hearers alike! The two witnesses will have miraculous power, to stop the rain (like Elijah; 1 Kings 17:1; James 5:17) and to bring fire upon their enemies (like Moses; Leviticus 10:1–3). But they will be

killed when their testimony is concluded. Their bodies will
lie in the streets for just over three days, while the multi-
national crowd, 'tormented' in conscience by their words,
gloat over and celebrate their removal. The relief will turn to
terror when the two are resurrected in full view of all. A loud
voice from heaven 'Come up here' will result in their
ascension. At the moment of their departure, a severe earthquake will destroy one-tenth of the city's buildings and 7,000
of its population.

The similarity between the fate of the two witnesses and
'the prophet' Jesus is striking. It will be impossible not to recall
his crucifixion, resurrection and ascension in this very same city.
Of course, there are differences: in his case, the earthquake
coincided with his death (Matthew 27:51) and neither his resurrection after three days nor his ascension were witnessed by
the general public. But it will still be a vivid reminder, especially
to the Jewish inhabitants, of those far-off days. It will result in
fear of, and glory to, God.

Who these two witnesses are, we are not told. All attempts
to identify them are sheer speculation. There is no suggestion
that they are 'reincarnate' figures from previous times, so they
are not Moses and Elijah, even though they are like them in
some ways, any more than they are two Jesuses, though they
are like him in others. We must 'wait and see' who they are,
but it obviously does not really matter. What they do and what
is done to them are the important things.

Before leaving this section, two 'anticipations' need to be
noted. For one thing, there is the first mention of a time period
of 1,260 days, which is 42 months, which is three and a half
years. We shall come across this figure in succeeding chapters,
where it seems to indicate the duration of the 'Big Trouble'.
Many link it with the 'half week' predicted by Daniel (Daniel
9:27; the New International Version rightly translates 'week' as

'seven'). It is quite a brief time and recalls Jesus' own prediction that it would be kept short (Matthew 24:22).

For another thing, this is the first mention of the 'beast', who figures so largely in the next parentheses in the ongoing narrative.

Chapters 12–14: the two beasts

To follow the literary pattern so far, this section should have come between the sixth and seventh bowls, but these follow each other so closely that there is neither time nor space between them for other events. So these three chapters are inserted before the seven bowls are poured out as the final expression of God's wrath on a rebellious world (see the diagram on page 196).

Six seals and six trumpets are over. The very last series of disasters is about to happen. It will be the worst for the world – and the toughest for the church. Evil powers will gain a tighter grip on society than they have ever had before, though their hold is about to be broken.

The section introduces three persons who form an alliance to rule the world themselves. One is angelic in origin and nature: a 'great dragon' and 'ancient serpent', otherwise known as 'Satan', or 'the devil' (12:9). The other two are human in origin and nature: 'beasts', otherwise known as 'the antichrist' (1 John 2:18; also 'the man of lawlessness' in 2 Thessalonians 2:3) and 'the false prophet' (16:13; 19:20; 20:10). Together they form a kind of 'unholy trinity' in a ghastly mimicry of God, Christ and the Holy Spirit.

Satan is introduced into the 'troubles' for the first time. He has not been mentioned in Revelation since the letters to the seven churches (2:9, 13, 24; 3:9). Seals and trumpets have loosed their burdens on the earth, while Satan has been in heaven. As an angel he has access to 'the heavenly realms'

(Ephesians 6:12; compare Job 1:6–7). That is where the real battle between good and evil is being fought out, as anyone entering these realms through prayer will discover.

This battle, between good and bad angels in heaven, will not last for ever. For one thing, the forces are unequal in number. The devil's side comprises one third of the heavenly host (12:4); the two thirds are led by the archangel Michael, who will lead his forces to victory (a sculpture portraying this conquest adorns the east wall of Coventry Cathedral).

The devil will be 'hurled' down to the earth. Later he will again be defeated and thrown into the 'abyss' (20:3). Meanwhile, in the few years he has left, his fury and frustration are concentrated on our planet. Unable to challenge God directly in heaven any more, he declares war on God's people below. It is a rearguard action, undertaken in the hope of retaining his kingdom on earth, through puppet rulers, one political and the other religious.

So far the message of chapter 12 is quite clear, even if it stretches the imagination. But we have overlooked (deliberately) the other major figure in the drama – a pregnant woman, bathed in sunshine, standing on the moon and wearing a crown of 12 stars on her head.

Who is she? Is she an individual person at all, or perhaps a 'personification' of a place or a people (as are the other 'women' in Revelation; for example, the 'prostitute' representing Babylon in chapters 17–18)?

Certainly, this figure has been the source of much debate and many differences among Bible students. For some, the matter is settled by the fact that the devil wanted to 'devour her child the moment it was born' (verse 4) and the statement that 'she gave birth to a son, a male child, who will rule all the nations with an iron sceptre' (verse 5). Surely, they say, this is an unmistakable reference to the birth of Jesus and Herod's immediate but abortive attempt to destroy him. The woman is therefore his mother, Mary (the usual Catholic interpretation); or a personification of Israel, from whom the Messiah came (a common Protestant interpretation to exclude Mary).

But it is not quite so simple as this. Why should there be a sudden and unexpected return to the very beginning of the Christian era in the middle of a passage describing the end times? Why bring Mary into the picture (after Acts 1 she disappears from the New Testament, her work completed). Of course, the 'cyclical historicists' see this as proof of yet another 'recapitulation' of the entire cycle of Church history, this time starting with the nativity, Satan being defeated and exiled from heaven at that time.

There are still problems. Apparently the child is 'snatched up to God and to his throne' almost immediately after his birth. This could be a 'telescoping' of the incarnation and ascension, but the absence of any reference to the ministry, death and resurrection of Jesus in between is at least striking. And if the woman is his mother, who are 'the rest of her offspring' to whom the frustrated dragon turns his attention (verse 17)? We know she had other children, including four boys and some girls (Mark 6:3), but they are unlikely candidates. Nor is it certain that 'ruling the nations with an iron sceptre' necessarily points to Jesus; it is applied to him (19:15, in fulfilment of Psalm 2:9), but it is also promised to his faithful followers (2:27). Then there is the preservation of the woman in 'the desert' for 1,260 days (12:6), a period which has already emerged as the duration of greatest distress at the end of the Church age.

The interpretation which best fits all this data sees the woman as a personification representing the Church in the end times, preserved outside urban areas during the worst troubles. Her man-child is also a personification, representing the martyred believers at this time, safe in heaven, out of Satan's reach. They will return to the earth one day and rule it with Christ (20:4 emphatically declares this). The 'rest of her offspring' are those who survive the holocaust, yet 'obey God's commandments and hold to the testimony of Jesus' (verse 17; compare 1:9; 14:12). There are still some tensions with the text in this view, but far fewer than with any other explanation.

Once again, there seems to be an implied comparison between the experience of Christ at the beginning of the Christian era and his followers at the end of it (as we saw earlier). In particular, as he 'overcame' (John 16:33) his followers will 'overcome', not 'loving their lives so much as to shrink from death' (12:11). Their victory demonstrates 'the kingdom of our God, and the authority of his Christ' (12:10; compare 11:15 and Acts 28:31).

The two 'beasts' arrive in chapter 13. The first and foremost is a political figure, a world dictator wielding a totalitarian regime over all known ethnic groupings. He is 'the antichrist' (1 John 2:18; note that *anti-* in Greek means 'instead of' rather than 'against', indicating a counterfeit rather than a competitor), 'the man of lawlessness' (2 Thessalonians 2:3–4) acknowledging no higher law than his own will and therefore claiming divinity and demanding worship. The beast is a human individual who accepts the satanic offer which Jesus refused (Matthew 4:8–9; had he accepted he would have become Jesus Antichrist!).

But he is also 'anti-Christian' in the other sense of that prefix. He has the power to 'make war against the saints and to *overcome* them' (13:7; he overcomes them temporarily, but they overcome him eternally, 12:11).

His characteristics are those of other fierce beasts – leopard, bear and lion. He seems to arise from a federation of political rulers, gaining the attention of the world through an astonishing recovery from a fatal wound, presumably in an attempted assassination. His blasphemous egotism is broadcast for 42 months.

His position is bolstered by the second beast, a religious colleague with supernatural power who focuses the world's worship on his superior. His miracles will deceive the nations as he commands fire to fall down from the sky and images of the dictator to speak.

His appearance will be 'like a lamb', a young sheep with only 'two horns'. This would seem to indicate mildness rather than Christlikeness, since it is contrasted with his dragon-like speech.

His master-stroke will not be his display of miracles but his domination of markets. Only those bearing a special number on a visible part of their body (hand or forehead) will be allowed to trade and the number will only be marked on those who engage in imperial idolatry. Jews and Christians will therefore be excluded from all commerce, even to the purchase of bare necessities of life.

The number '666' is the coded name of the dictator. We have already discussed its meaning (see page 156). Until he arrives, when his identity with this figure will be only too obvious, all attempts to decode it are useless speculation. One thing is clear, he will fall short of perfection (7) in every regard.

Chapter 14 seems to compensate for these horrific scenes by turning our attention to a group of people standing (literally) in sharp contrast to those who have allowed themselves to be entrapped in the system. Instead of the cryptic name of the beast, they carry the Lamb's Father's name on their foreheads (another feature picked up in 22:4). Instead of the arrogant lies, they are known for integrity of speech, as well as pure sexual relations.

There is a little uncertainty about their location, whether in heaven or on earth, but the context favours the former, because of the songs of praise from living creatures and elders (14:3 seems to repeat 4:4–11), songs which only the redeemed can 'learn', much less sing. The number (144,000) is puzzling. It is not to be confused with the same number in chapter 7. There it referred to Jews on earth, here to Christians in heaven. There it was made up from 12 tribes, here it is not. Neither can it be equated with the 'great multitude that no one could count' in that same chapter. Again, it may be a 'round' number. But the clue probably lies in their being 'purchased from among men and offered as *firstfruits* to God and the Lamb' (verse 4). They are only the small foretaste of a very large harvest. So the point may be that what is the total number of Jews preserved on earth is only a partial number of Christians praising in heaven.

The rest of the chapter has a procession of angels bringing various messages from God to men:

The first calls for the fear and worship of God, with a reminder that the gospel is still available to save anyone from the 'coming wrath' (Luke 3:7).

The second announces the fall of Babylon. Here is another 'anticipation', since this is the first time such a place has been mentioned. All will be made clear in the next section (chapters 16–17).

The third warns believers of the terrible consequences of giving in to the pressures of the final totalitarian system. The language is that of hell: unceasing 'torment' (the same word describing the experience of the devil, the antichrist and the false prophet in the 'lake of fire'; 20:10). In other words, they will share the fate of those to whom they have surrendered. The fact that 'saints' could find themselves in this dreadful destiny is underlined by a call to 'patient endurance' immediately after the warning (verse 12, which repeats 13:10). Both contexts recognize that some will pay for their loyalty with their lives. For them a special beatitude is written: 'Blessed are the dead who die in [the sense is almost 'for'] the Lord from now on' (verse 13). The blessing is twofold: they can now rest from travail and, since the record of their loyalty has been kept, look forward to a reward. Even those who die of natural causes at that time will enjoy this blessing. But this verse should not yet be used at funerals; the promise is qualified by 'from now on', which refers to the reign of the 'beast'.

The fourth shouts to someone 'like a son of man on the clouds' (a clear reference to Daniel 7:13), telling him it is high time for harvest time. Whether this is to gather tares for burning or wheat for storing (Matthew 13:40–43) is not immediately clear.

The fifth simply appears with a sickle in his hand.

The sixth directs the sickle to 'grapes' which are to be trampled on in the 'great winepress of God's wrath', which is 'outside the city'. That this refers to a mass slaughter of human beings is indicated by the massive pool of blood (a metre deep over 180 square miles – surely a touch of hyperbole?). This is probably an anticipation of the battle of Armageddon, where vultures will clean up the corpses (19:17–21). In passing, we note this link between blood, wine and God's wrath, which occurs quite frequently. This throws a flood of light on the cross and particularly on the agonizing prayer in 'Gethsemane', which means 'crushing'. The metaphorical use of 'cup' in Scripture invariably refers to God's wrath (Isaiah 51:21–22; Mark 14:36; Revelation 16:19).

These six angels are followed by seven more who act out rather than speak about the outpoured wrath of God. They carry seven bowls, not just cups, of wrath to tip on the earth. This is accompanied by a song of triumph from the martyrs in heaven, consciously echoing the rejoicing of Moses after the Egyptian forces were drowned in the Red Sea (15:2–4). The theme is the justice and righteousness of God, expressed in great and marvellous deeds which vindicate his holiness by punishing the oppressors. The 'King of the Ages' may take his time to judge the guilty, but judgement is certain to come – and at last has come.

Before we leave this major middle section of Revelation, two further observations must be made.

The first concerns the *order* of events. An attempt has been made to fit the seals, trumpets and bowls, together with the inserted parentheses, into some kind of consecutive schedule. Whether this has been successful must be judged by the reader, who may have already worked out a different scheme.

The fact is that it is extremely difficult, if not impossible, to fit all the predicted events into a coherent pattern. But Jesus is too good a teacher to hide his essential message in such a complex narrative. What does this tell us?

Simply this: *the order is not the primary thrust* in this section. It is far more concerned with what will happen than with when anything will happen. The purpose of it all is not to enable us to become accurate soothsayers, able to forecast the future, but to be faithful servants of the Lord, ready to face the worst that can happen to us. But will it happen to us?

The second concerns the *fulfilment* of predictions. If the 'Big Trouble' only covers the last few years, it may be that we shall not have to face it in our lifetime. So could it be a waste of time for all but the last generation of saints to prepare for it?

One answer is that the current trend and speed of world events makes it an increasing possibility in the near future.

But the main response to this kind of thinking must be the reminder that future events cast their shadows before them. 'Dear children, this is the last hour; and as you have heard that the antichrist is coming, even now many antichrists have come'

(1 John 2:18). The false prophet is coming, but even now many false prophets have come (Matthew 24:11; Acts 13:6; Revelation 2:20).

In other words, what will one day be experienced by the whole church on a universal scale ('hated by all nations'; Matthew 24:9) is already happening in local and regional settings. Any Christian can go through much tribulation before all go through the 'Great Tribulation'. We must all be ready for the kind of troubles that reach a climax then, but can come now.

This section (chapters 6–16) is therefore directly relevant to all believers, whatever their contemporary situation. The church is already under pressure in the majority of countries and the number of those where this is not the case diminishes annually.

And beyond all this lies the return of the Lord Jesus Christ, for which every believer needs to be ready. The main motive for preparing to be faithful under pressure is to be able to face him without shame. Perhaps that explains the following reminder inserted between the sixth and seventh bowls of wrath (incidentally, confirming that some Christians will still be on earth at that time): 'Behold, I come like a thief! Blessed is he who stays awake and keeps his clothes with him, so that he may not go naked and be shamefully exposed' (16:15; note the same emphasis on attire in Matthew 22:11; Luke 12:35; Revelation 19:7–8).

Chapters 17–18: Man on Earth

This section is still part of the 'Big Trouble', but only just. It concerns the very end, at the time of the severe earthquake in the seventh seal, trumpet and bowl (see 16:17–19).

World history is hastening to an end. The final denouement is at hand. In spite of all the warnings, whether in divine word or deed, human beings still refuse to repent and curse God for all their troubles (16:9, 11, 21).

The remainder of Revelation is dominated by two female figures, one a filthy prostitute and the other a pure bride. Neither is a person; both are personifications. They represent cities.

We could use the title: 'A tale of two cities'. They are Babylon and Jerusalem, the city of man and the city of God. In this section we consider the former, which has been mentioned already (14:8; 16:19).

Cities are generally regarded as bad places in the Bible. The first mention (which is usually significant) associates them with the line of Lamech and the manufacture of weapons for mass destruction. They concentrate people, therefore sinners, therefore sin. With less community and more anonymity, vice and crime flourish. There is more lust (prostitution) and anger (violence) in urban than rural communities.

The two sins that are singled out here are greed and pride. Both are related to the idolatry of money. Since it is impossible to worship both God and Mammon (Luke 16:13), it is easier to forget the Maker of heaven and earth in a prosperous city. Self-made men worship their own creator! Arrogance shows in architecture; buildings are often monuments to human ambition and achievement.

Such was the tower of Babel by the Euphrates river, sitting on the route between Asia, Africa and Europe. Founded by Nimrod the mighty hunter (of animals) and warrior (among men), it was founded on the belief that might is right, that the fittest survive.

Typically, the tower was to be the tallest man-made structure in the world, as an impressive statement both to men and God. The expressed intention to 'make a name for ourselves' (Genesis 11:4) marks the beginning of humanism, man's self-deification. God judged this presumption by granting its inhabitants the gift of tongues! But the simultaneous removal of their common speech brought unintelligible bedlam, from which we derive the verb 'babble' (note that at Pentecost this did not happen, for the same gift brought unity; Acts 2:44).

This city later became the capital of a large and powerful empire, especially under Nebuchadnezzar, a ruthless tyrant who destroyed babies, animals and even trees when conquering new territory (Habakkuk 2:17; 3:17).

Meanwhile, King David of Israel had established Jerusalem as his capital. By contrast, it was not in a strategic position for trade, since it was not by the sea, a major river or a main road. It was, however, the 'city of God', the place where he put his name and chose to live among his people – at first in the tent Moses assembled, later in the temple Solomon built.

Babylon became the greatest threat to Jerusalem. Nebuchadnezzar ultimately destroyed the holy city, with its temple, transporting its treasures and deporting its people into 70 years of exile. God allowed this to happen because the inhabitants had made it an 'unholy' city like all others.

But this was a temporary chastisement rather than a permanent punishment. Through the prophets God promised both the restoration of Jerusalem and the ruin of Babylon (for example, Isaiah 13:19–20; Jeremiah 51:6–9, 45–48). Sure enough, that evil city became a desolate heap of rubble, totally uninhabited, except by wild creatures of the desert, exactly as foretold.

It is no coincidence that there are profound similarities between the books of Daniel and Revelation. Both contain visions of the end times that are in remarkable agreement. Yet the revelations were given to Daniel during the time of Nebuchadnezzar (he had been a young man in the first of three deportations). He had 'seen' the future course of world empires right up to the time of Christ and then beyond, to the very end of history, the reign of antichrist, the millennial rule, the resurrection of the dead and the Day of Judgement.

Both books talk about a city called 'Babylon'. But are they talking about the same place?

If so, it will have to be rebuilt. Those who take the Revelation 'Babylon' as the very same are quite excited that parts of it have already been rebuilt by the present President of Iraq, Saddam Hussein. But he seems to have no intention of restoring it as a living city; it is more a showcase for his own prestige (laser lights project his profile, alongside Nebuchadnezzar's, on to the clouds!). It is highly unlikely that ancient Babylon, even fully rebuilt, could ever become a strategic centre again.

The 'preterist' school of interpretation applies 'Babylon' to the metropolis of Rome. There is some ground for doing so, not least because this was probably the way original readers of Revelation would take it. One of Peter's letters, written for a very similar purpose (to prepare saints for suffering), may already have made this coded link (1 Peter 5:13). And the reference to 'seven hills' would probably clinch it (17:9, though note that the 'hills' represent kings).

Rome's decadent character would also fit the description in Revelation. Her seductive attraction of goods and finance in return for favours rendered and her domination of petty kings fit the picture well.

Yet it is doubtful if this is the total fulfilment. Rome was certainly *a* Babylon. But it was only a foreshadowing of *the* Babylon which dominates the end of history, which is where Revelation firmly places it.

Some have resolved the problem by postulating a revived Roman Empire. Their pulses quickened when 10 nations (17:12) signed the 'Treaty of Rome' as the basis for a new superpower, the European Community. Interest has subsided with the addition of other states; there are now too many 'horns'! But the flag has the 12 stars of Revelation 12.

The reluctance to let go of Rome as the main candidate is also apparent in the 'historicist' school of interpretation. Taking Revelation as an overview of the whole of Church history, Protestants invariably fastened on the papacy and the Vatican, with their claims to political as well as religious power, as the 'scarlet woman' of Babylon (this identification has created havoc in the 'troubles' of Northern Ireland). Catholics returned the compliment and regarded the Protestant Reformers in a similar light!

Actually, there is no hint in Revelation that 'Babylon' is in any way a religious centre. The emphasis is on business and pleasure as the primary occupations of its inhabitants.

The 'futurist' school seems to be nearer the truth in seeing the city as a new metropolis rising to dominate others during the 'end time'. Since it is designated a 'mystery' (i.e. a secret now revealed), it would appear to be a fresh creation of man rather than the re-establishment of a former city (whether ancient Babylon or Rome).

It is clearly going to be a, even the, centre of commerce, a place for getting and spending money (note how the traders are affected by its downfall; 18:11–16). Culture will not be neglected (note the music in 18:22).

But it will be corrupt and corrupting, characterized by materialism without morality, pleasure without purity, wealth without wisdom, lust without love. The simile of the harlot is peculiarly appropriate, giving anyone what they want in exchange for money.

So far we have only considered the 'woman', but she rides a 'beast' with seven heads and ten horns, which clearly represent a federation of political figures. We are not told who they are, nor are we given many details about them. They are powerful men but without territory to rule. Their authority derives from the 'beast', presumably the antichrist, to whom they will devote absolute allegiance. Above all, they will be blatantly anti-Christian, making 'war against the Lamb' and those 'with him' (17:14), presumably because their consciences will be pricked.

But Babylon is doomed. She and they will fall. Their days will be numbered. The astonishing way in which this is brought about is entirely credible in the modern world.

The woman rides the beast. A queen is riding on the backs of kings (a reversal of gender contrary to creation). It is another way of saying that economics will rule politics, that the power of money will override other authority. Since by the year AD 2000 the bulk of the world's business was in the hands of 300 colossal corporations, this scenario is not difficult to imagine.

Amtibious politicians, hungry for power, resent this financial clout. They are even prepared to bring about economic disaster if that will enable them to take over. One thinks of Hitler's treatment of the Jews, who controlled many banks in Germany.

The 'kings' will be jealous of the 'woman' who rides them and will resolve to destroy her. The city will be razed by fire. It will be the biggest economic disaster the world will have seen. Many, many people will 'weep and mourn' over the ruins.

God will have caused the catastrophe, but not by any physical action. He will have 'put it into their hearts to accomplish his purpose' (17:17). He will have encouraged them to make an alliance with the beast against the city. The antichrist will have political control and the false prophet religious control; the 'kings' will now offer them economic control in return for delegated powers for themselves. But their enjoyment of such privileges will be extremely brief ('one hour'; 17:12).

So sure is Babylon's downfall that it is pictured in Revelation as already having happened. Christians can be absolutely certain of this. But there are practical reasons why they are being told about it. What is the relation between God's people and this last 'Babylon'? Three guidelines are given:

First, there will be many martyrs in the city. The whore is 'drunk with the blood of the saints, the blood of those who bore testimony to Jesus'. This last phrase again indicates the presence of Christians and occurs throughout Revelation (1:9; 12:17; 14:12; 17:6; 19:10; 20:4). There is no place for holy people in a city devoted to immorality. The community does not want a conscience.

Second, the Christians are told to 'come out of her, my people, so that you will not share in her sins, so that you will not receive any of her plagues, for her sins are piled up to heaven, and God has remembered her crimes' (18:4–5). This is almost identical to Jeremiah's plea to Jews in ancient Babylon (Jeremiah 51:6). Note that they have to 'come out'; the Lord does not take them out. Clearly, not all believers will be martyred; some will escape with their lives, though they may have to leave their money and possessions behind.

Third, when Babylon falls, a celebration is commanded: 'Rejoice over her, O heaven! Rejoice, saints and apostles and prophets! God has judged her for the way she treated you' (18:20). This is done in 19:1–5. Very few realize that the famous 'Hallelujah' chorus in Handel's *Messiah* oratorio is a celebration of the collapse of the world economy, the closure of stock exchanges, the bankruptcy of banks and the disruption of trade and commerce! Only God's people will be singing 'Hallelujah' (which means: 'Praise the Lord') on that day!

The prostitute disappears and the bride appears. The 'wedding supper of the Lamb' is about to take place. Jesus is going to get married – rather, he's coming to get married (Matthew 25:1–13). The bride has 'made herself ready' by acquiring a dress of pure white linen (note the 'clothes' reference again); this is explained as a symbol of 'the righteous acts of the saints' (19:8). The guest list is completed and 'blessed' are those on it.

We have already strayed into chapter 19, which leads into the next section, while rounding off this one. But then the chapter divisions were not part of the original text and often come in the wrong places, putting asunder what God has joined together, never more so than in the penultimate section of Revelation.

Chapters 19–20: Christ on Earth

This series of events brings history, as we know it, to a close. Our world is brought to an end at last. We are now dealing with the ultimate future.

Alas, this section has given rise to more controversy than any other in the whole book, mainly centred on the Millennium, the repeated mention of a 'thousand years'. This is such an important issue that it will be dealt with as a separate subject. That treatment will include an exhaustive exegesis of the text, so no more than a summary will be given here.

It is vital to note the change from verbal to visual revelations. Throughout the previous section John says: 'I heard' (18:4; 19:1, 6). Then the phrase becomes a repeated: 'I saw', until it changes back to 'I heard' again (in 21:3).

When the visual part is analysed, a series of seven visions is clearly discerned. But for the unwarranted intrusion of chapter divisions ('20' and '21'), this sevenfold revelation would have been noticed by most readers. As it is, few have marked it. Yet it is the final 'seven' in Revelation. As with previous sevens, the first four belong together, the next two are less closely related and the last stands on its own (we shall postpone study of it until we look at chapters 21–22). They may be listed as follows:

1. Parousia (19:11–16)
   King of kings, Lord of lords (and *logos* = 'word')
   White horses, blood-stained robes

2. Supper (19:17–18)
   Angelic invitation to birds ...
   ... to gorge on corpses

3. Armageddon (19:19–21)
   Kings and armies destroyed (by 'word' = *logos*)
   Two beasts thrown into the lake of fire

4. Satan (20:1–3)
   Bound and banished to 'abyss'
   But for limited time

5. Millennium (20:4–10)
   Saints and martyrs reign (first resurrection)
   Satan released and thrown into the lake of fire

6. Judgement (20:11–15)
   General resurrection of 'the rest'
   Books and 'book of life' opened

7. Re-creation (21:1–2)
   New heaven and earth
   New Jerusalem

Clearly this indicates a consecutive series of events, beginning
with the Second Coming and ending with the new creation.
This is confirmed by internal cross-references (e.g. 20:10
refers back to 19:20). Unfortunately, commentators have tried
to disrupt the sequence in the interests of a theological system

(by claiming that chapter 20 precedes chapter 19, for example). But the order in these last chapters is far clearer than the middle of Revelation – and it is very significant.

For example, the enemies of the people of God are expelled from the scene in reverse order to their introduction. Satan appears in chapter 12, the two 'beasts' in chapter 13 and Babylon in chapter 17. Babylon disappears in chapter 18, the two 'beasts' in chapter 19 and Satan in chapter 20. The city falls before the return of Christ, but he is needed on earth to deal with the 'unholy trinity' of devil, antichrist and false prophet.

The opening vision is acknowledged to be a picture of the Second Coming by almost all scholars (only a few, for vested theological interests, say it refers to his First). But Jesus' return to earth will cause consternation in the powers-that-be. Shocked by his reappearance, they will plan a second assassination. But this time a small platoon of guards will be totally inadequate, since millions of his devoted followers will have met him in Jerusalem (1 Thessalonians 4:14–17). A huge military force will gather some miles north in the valley of Esdraelon at the foot of the 'mountain of Megiddo' (in Hebrew, Har-mageddon): it is the crossroads of the world, overlooked by Nazareth. Many battles have been fought here; many kings have died here (Saul and Josiah among them).

Jesus only needs a 'word' to raise the dead or kill the living. It is more a sentence than a struggle. Vultures deal with the bodies, too many to bury.

At this point, there are a number of surprising developments. The two 'beasts' are not killed but 'thrown alive' into hell, the first human beings to go there. The devil is not sent there, but taken into custody – to be released again later!

Above all, Jesus does not then bring this world to an end, but takes over the government himself, filling the political

vacuum left by the 'unholy trinity' with his own faithful followers, especially the martyrs. They will, of course, have to be
raised from the dead to fulfil this responsibility. This
'Kingdom' will last for a thousand years but come to an end
when a paroled devil deceives the nations into a final but
abortive rebellion, put down by fire from heaven. This interim
between Jesus' return and the Day of Judgement is widely
rejected in the Church today, yet it was the accepted view of
the early Church.

There is widespread agreement on what follows. A final
day of reckoning is clearly taught throughout the New
Testament. It is heralded by two remarkable portents. The
earth and sky disappear. We know (from 2 Peter 3:10) that
both will be 'razed' by fire. The dead, including those lost at
sea, reappear. This is the second, or 'general' resurrection
(20:5) and confirms that the wicked as well as the righteous will
be re-embodied before entering their eternal destiny (Daniel
12:2; John 5:29; Acts 24:15). Both 'soul and body' will be
thrown into the lake of fire (Matthew 10:28; Revelation 19:20).
The 'torment' will be physical as well as mental (Luke
16:23–24). Therefore, both 'death', which separates body from
spirit, and 'hades', the abode of disembodied spirits, are now
abolished (20:14). The 'second death', which neither separates
body and soul nor annihilates either, takes over from then on.

All that is now visible are the judge sitting on a throne, the
judged standing before it and an enormous pile of books. The
throne is large and white, representing absolute power and
purity. It is probably not the same throne as the one John saw
in heaven (4:2–4). That was not described as 'great' or 'white'.
Furthermore, it is most unlikely that the resurrected wicked
would be allowed anywhere near heaven. Indeed, there is no
hint that the scene in chapter 20 has shifted back to heaven; it
is more likely to be located where the earth has been, the earth

having disappeared leaving only its past and present inhabitants. Above all, the person sitting on this throne is not identified as God (as in 4:8–11). It is, in fact, not God. From other scriptures, we know that he has delegated the task of judging the human race to his Son, Jesus: 'For he has set a day when he will judge the world with justice by the man he has appointed' (Acts 17:31; compare Matthew 25:31–32; 2 Corinthians 5:10). Human beings will be judged by a human being.

This will be no long drawn-out trial. All the evidence has already been gathered and examined by the judge. It is contained in 'books', volumes truly deserving the title: 'This is Your Life'! They will not be a selection of the commendable occasions for a television presentation, but a complete record of the deeds (and words; Matthew 5:22; 12:36) of a whole lifetime, from birth to death. We may be justified by faith, but we shall be judged by works.

If this was all the evidence to be considered, it would damn us all to the 'second death'. What hope would there be for any? Thank God, one other book will be opened on that terrible day. It is the record of the judge's own life on earth, both absolving him and qualifying him to judge others. It is the 'Lamb's book of life' (21:27). But it contains other names besides his. Those who are 'in Christ' are listed there, those who have lived and died in him, those who have been joined to and have remained in this 'true vine' (John 15:1–8). They have thus borne the fruit that attests their continuing union with him (Philippians 4:3; contrast Matthew 7:16–20). The fruitfulness is proof of their faithfulness.

Their names have been put into this book when they came to be in Christ, when they repented and believed (the phrase 'from the creation of the world' in 17:8 refers to those whose names are *not* written in the book and simply means 'through the whole of human history'; likewise in 13:8 though the phrase there may be linked to the slaying of the Lamb). Their names have not been 'erased' from the book of life because they have 'overcome' (3:5).

Only those whose names are still in this book escape the 'second death' in the 'lake of fire'. In other words, outside of Christ there is no hope whatsoever, since 'all have sinned and fall short of the glory of God' (Romans 3:23). The gospel is therefore *exclusive:* 'Salvation is found in no one else, for there is no other name [except 'Jesus'] under heaven given to men by which we must be saved' (Acts 4:12). But it must also therefore be *inclusive:* 'Go into all the world and preach the good news to all creation' (Mark 16:15; compare Matthew 28:19; Luke 24:47).

The human race will then be permanently divided into two groups (Matthew 13:41–43, 47–50; 25:32–33). For one, their destination has already been 'prepared' (Matthew 25:41). The lake (or 'sea') of fire has been in existence for at least a thousand years (Revelation 19:20). For the other, a new metropolis has been 'prepared' (John 14:2), but there is no earth on which it may be sited, much less a sky above it. A new universe is needed.

Chapters 21–22: Heaven on Earth

It is with great relief that we enter this final section. The atmosphere has changed dramatically. The dark clouds have rolled away and the sun is shining again – except that the sun has also disappeared, to be replaced by the much more brilliant glory of God (21:23).

This is the final act of redemption, bringing salvation to the entire universe. This is the 'cosmic' work of Christ (Matthew 19:28; Acts 3:21; Romans 8:18–25; Colossians 1:20; Hebrews 2:8), the renewal of heaven and earth (note that 'heaven' means 'sky', what we call 'space'; it is the same word in

20:11 and 21:1). Christians have already received new bodies, when Jesus came back to the old earth. Now they are to be given a new environment corresponding to their new bodies.

The first two verses cover the last vision in the sequence of seven which John 'saw' (19:11 to 21:2), the climax to the final events of history. There is more than a new universe here. Within the 'general' creation is a 'special' creation. Just as within the first universe God 'planted a garden' (Genesis 2:8), so here he has designed and built a 'garden city', which even Abraham knew about and looked forward to (Hebrews 11:10).

Just as the new 'heaven and earth' are recognizably similar enough to the old to bear the same names, this city is given the same name as David's capital. Jerusalem has a place in the New Testament as well as the Old. Jesus called it 'the city of the Great King' (Matthew 5:35; compare Psalm 48:2). It was just 'outside a city wall' that he died, rose again and ascended to heaven. It is to this city that he will return to sit on the throne of David. In the Millennium it will be 'the camp of God's people, the city he loves' (20:9).

Of course, the earthly city was in a sense a temporary replica of 'the heavenly Jerusalem, the city of the living God', of which all believers in Jesus are already citizens, together with Hebrew saints and angels (Hebrews 12:22–23). But that does not mean that the original is somehow less real than the copy, that one is material and the other 'spiritual'. The main difference between them is one of location. And that will change.

The heavenly city will come 'down out of heaven' and be sited on the new earth. It will be a real city, a material construction, though of rather different materials! Unfortunately, ever since Augustine's Platonic separation of the physical and spiritual realms, the Church has had real difficulties in accepting the concept of a new earth, never mind a new city on it.

The equation of 'spiritual' and 'intangible' has done immense damage to Christian hopes for the future. This new universe and its metropolis will not be less 'material' than the old.

Verses 3–8 are an explanatory comment on this final vision. The attention is immediately diverted from the new creation to its Creator. Note the transition from what John 'saw' to what he 'heard'. But whose 'loud voice' did he hear? It speaks of God in the third person, then in the first. This is surely Christ speaking (compare 1:15). The phrase 'seated on' the throne is the same as in the previous chapter (compare 20:11 with 21:5). In both contexts judgement is expressed and the 'lake of fire' mentioned (compare 20:15 with 21:8). Above all, the identical claim is made by this 'voice' as Jesus makes in the epilogue (compare 21:6 with 22:13). However, the 'throne of God and of the Lamb' are later seen as one (22:1).

Three startling statements follow:

The first is the most remarkable revelation about the future in the whole book. God himself is changing his residence from heaven to earth! He will come to live with human beings at their address, no longer 'our Father in heaven' (Matthew 6:9), but 'our Father on earth', leading to the most intimate relationship ever between human and divine persons. Since all death, sorrow and pain are contrary to his nature, they will have no place. There will be no more separation, no more tears. In passing, we recall the only other mention of God on earth in the Bible: his evening stroll in the garden of Eden (Genesis 3:8). Once again, the Bible has come full circle.

The second is the announcement that 'I am making everything new' (Revelation 21:5). Here the carpenter of Nazareth claims to be the Creator of the new universe, as he was of the old (John 1:3; Hebrews 1:2). His work is not limited to regenerating people, though that also is 'the new creation' (2 Corinthians 5:17). He is restoring all things as well.

There is considerable debate about the word 'new'. How new is 'new'? Is this 'new' universe simply the old one 'renovated' or a brand new manufacture? There certainly are two Greek words for 'new' (*kainos* and *eos*), but they are somewhat synonymous and the use of the former here does not settle the issue. References to the old universe as being 'destroyed by fire' (2 Peter 3:10) and having 'passed away' (Revelation 21:1) suggest eradication rather than transformation. But the process has already begun – with the resurrection of Jesus. His 'old' body dissolved inside the graveclothes and he came from death with a new 'glorious' body (Philippians 3:21); see also my book *Explaining the Resurrection* (Sovereign World, 1993). The exact 'connection' between the two bodies is hidden in the darkness of the tomb, but what happened there will one day happen on a universal scale.

The third spells out the practical implications of this new creation for the readers of Revelation (note that John has had to be reminded to keep writing down what he is hearing because 'these words are trustworthy and true'; 21:5). On the positive side is the promise to satisfy the thirst of those seeking 'the water of life' (21:6; 22:1, 17). But this must lead on to an 'overcoming' life, in order to inherit a place in the new earth and enjoy the family relationship with God in it.

On the negative side is the warning that those who do not overcome, but are cowardly, faithless, immoral and deceitful, will never be part of all this, but end up in 'the fiery lake of burning sulphur. This is the second death' (21:8). It needs to be pointed out that this warning is given to wayward believers, not unbelievers, as is the whole book. Most of Jesus' earlier warnings about hell were addressed, not to sinners, but to his own disciples (see my book *The Road to Hell*, Hodder and Stoughton, 1992).

At this point an angel takes John on a conducted tour of the New Jerusalem and its life (the idea that what follows is actually a 'recapitulation' of the 'old' Jerusalem in the Millennium is so bizarre we shall not consider it; verse 10 clearly expands verse 2). The description is breathtaking, straining vocabulary to the limit, which raises a fundamental question: how much is literal and how much is symbolical?

On the one hand, taking it entirely literally seems wrong. Clearly, John is describing the indescribable (Paul had the same difficulty when shown heavenly realities; 2 Corinthians 12:4). Notice how often he can only use a comparison ('like' or 'as' in 21:11, 18, 21; 22:1), yet all analogies are only approximate and ultimately inadequate. But the realities imperfectly portrayed here must be more wonderful than this, not less.

On the other hand, taking it entirely symbolically also seems wrong. Taken to this extreme, the whole picture dissolves into 'spiritual' unreality, which fails to do justice to the 'new earth' as the clear location.

To highlight the problem, we may ask the question: does the New Jerusalem represent a place or a people? The question arises because she is called a 'bride', which previously indicated a people, the Church (in 19:7–8). At first, this is only an analogy (in 21:3; '*as* a bride') and anyone who has seen a Semitic wedding will understand the likeness of the highly coloured clothes bedecked with jewellery. Later, however, the city is specifically designated 'the bride, the wife of the Lamb' (21:9). The angel, promising to *show* 'the bride' to John, *shows* him the city (21:10), though the vision moves on to reveal the life of its inhabitants (21:24–22:5).

The answer to the dilemma is much more obvious to a Jew than a Christian. 'Israel', the bride of Yahweh, was always a people *and* a place, inextricably involved with each other, hence all the prophetic promises of the ultimate restoration of the people to their own land. By comparison, Christians are a people without a place here, strangers, pilgrims, sojourners passing through, the new 'diaspora' or dispersed and exiled people of God (James 1:1; 1 Peter 1:1). Heaven is our 'home'. But heaven is coming down to earth at the last. Jew and Gentile will together be the people with a place. That is why the names on the city are the 12 tribes and the 12 apostles (21:12–14).

This dual unifying of Jew and Gentile, heaven and earth, is fundamental to God's eternal purpose 'to bring all things … together under one head, even Christ' (Ephesians 1:10; Colossians 1:20). So the 'bride', who becomes one both in herself and with her husband, is a people and a place. And what a place!

The measurements are clearly important, all multiples of 12. The *size* is enormous: over 2,000 kilometres in each of three dimensions; the city would cover most of Europe or just fit into the moon if it were hollow. In other words, big enough to accommodate all God's people. The *shape* is also significant, more like a cube than a pyramid, indicating a 'holy' city like the cubed 'holy of holies' in tabernacle and temple. The walls define the outside rather than defend the inside, since the gates are always open. There is no threatened danger so its inhabitants can freely leave and return at any time.

The materials used in its construction are already known to us, but only as rare and precious gemstones which give us a tiny glimpse of heaven. The list here is one of the most remarkable proofs of the divine inspiration of this book. Now that we can produce 'purer' light (polarized and laser), a hitherto unknown quality of precious stones has been revealed. When thin sections are exposed to cross-polarized light (as when two lenses from sun-glasses are superimposed at right angles), they fall into two very distinct categories. 'Isotropic' stones lose all their colour, for they depend on random rays for their brilliance (e.g. diamonds, rubies and garnets). 'Anisotropic' stones produce all the colours of the rainbow in dazzling patterns, whatever their original colour. *All* the stones in the New Jerusalem belong to this latter category! No one could possibly have known this when Revelation was written – except God himself!

Another striking feature of this description is that in just 32 verses there are over 50 allusions to the Old Testament (mainly from Genesis, Psalms, Isaiah, Ezekiel and Zechariah). Every major feature is, in fact, the fulfilment of Jewish hopes expressed in prophecy. This also indicates that Old and New Testament prophecies all spring from the same source (1 Peter 1:11; 2 Peter 1:21). Revelation is the climax and conclusion to the whole Bible.

When the angelic demonstration moves on to the life enjoyed by the inhabitants of the city, there are some surprises. Perhaps the biggest contrast to the 'old' Jerusalem is the absence of a dominating temple to focus worship at a particular place (or at a particular time?). The whole city *is* his temple, in which the redeemed 'serve him day and night' (Revelation 7:15), which suggests that work and worship have been blended together again, as they were for Adam (Genesis 2:15; Adam was not told to have one day in seven for worship).

The city will be enriched with international culture (Revelation 21:24, 26). It will never be polluted with immoral behaviour (21:27). That is why compromised believers are in danger of having their names erased from 'the Lamb's book of life' (3:5; 21:7–8).

The river and tree of life will ensure continuous health. As at the beginning, the diet will be fruit rather than meat (Genesis 1:29), though there is no obligation to be vegetarian before then (Genesis 9:3; Romans 14:2; 1 Timothy 4:3).

Above all, the saints will live in the presence of God. They will actually see his face, a privilege given to few before (Genesis 32:30; Exodus 33:11) but then to all (1 Corinthians 13:12). They will reflect him in their own faces, his name on their foreheads, as once others bore the number of the 'beast' (Revelation 13:16). They will 'reign for ever and ever', presumably over the new creation rather than each other, as was originally intended (Genesis 1:28). In this way they will 'serve' the Creator.

Once again, it needs to be emphasized that human beings have not gone to heaven to be with the Lord for ever; he has come to earth to be with them for ever. The New Jerusalem is at once the eternal divine and human 'dwelling-place', their permanent residence.

As before, John has to be reminded to write it all down. His distraction from the task is understandable!

The 'epilogue' (Revelation 22:7–21) has much in common with the 'prologue' (1:1–8). The same title is applied to God in one and Christ in the other (1:8; 22:13). This concluding exhortation is thoroughly trinitarian: God, the Lamb and the Spirit are all present.

There is a strong emphasis on the fact that time is short. Jesus is coming 'soon' (22:7, 12, 20). The fact that many centuries have elapsed since this was said and written should not lead to complacency; we must be much nearer 'the things that must soon take place' (22:6).

The day of opportunity is still here. The thirsty may still drink the water of life as a free gift (22:17). But choices must be made now. The time is coming when the moral direction of our lives will be fixed for ever (22:11). Pharaoh hardened his heart against the Lord seven times, so then God hardened it for him three times (Exodus 7–11; Romans 9:17–18). There will come a point when this happens to all who defy and disobey his will.

There are only two categories of people in the end: those who 'go on washing their robes' (Revelation 22:17; compare 7:14) and thus enter the city – and those kept outside it (22:15), like the wild curs of the Middle East today. This is now the third time a list of disqualifying offences has been included in this sublime finale (21:8, 27; 22:15), as if the readers must never be allowed to forget that the glories of the future will not come to them automatically because they have believed in Jesus and belong to a church, but to those who 'press on towards the goal to win the prize for which God has called us heavenwards in Christ Jesus' (Philippians 3:14) and who 'make every effort ... to be holy, for without holiness no one will see the Lord' (Hebrews 12:14).

Another way in which believers can forfeit the future is by tampering with this Book of Revelation, either by addition or subtraction. Since it is a 'prophecy', God speaking through his servant, to alter it in any way is to commit sacrilege, incurring the severest penalty. It is unlikely that unbelievers would even bother to do this. It is much more likely to be done by those who take upon themselves the task of explaining and interpreting it to others. May God have mercy on this poor author if he has offended in this way!

But the final note is positive, not negative, and is summed up in one word: 'Come!'

On the one hand, this invitation on the lips of the Church is addressed to the world, to 'whoever' will respond to the gospel (Revelation 22:17; compare John 3:16). On the other hand, it is addressed to the Lord: 'Amen. Come, Lord Jesus' (22:10).

This dual plea is characteristic of the true bride who is moved by the Spirit (22:17) and is experiencing the grace of the Lord Jesus (22:21). All the saints cry: 'Come!', both to the renegade world and its returning Lord.

The centrality of Christ

This last book of the Bible is 'the revelation of Jesus Christ' (1:1). The genitive ('of') can be understood in two ways: It is *from* him or *about* him. Perhaps the double meaning is intended. Either way he is central to its message.

If the theme is the end of the world, he is 'the end', as he was 'the beginning' (22:13). God's plan is 'to bring all things in heaven and on earth together under one head, even Christ' (Ephesians 1:10).

The prologue and epilogue both focus on his return to planet earth (1:7; 22:20). The hinge on which future history swings from getting worse to getting better is that second coming (19:11–16).

It is 'this same Jesus' (Acts 1:11) who will return. He is the Lamb of God who came the first time to take away 'the sin of the world' (John 1:29). Throughout Revelation the Lamb looks 'as if it had been slain' (5:6). Presumably the scars will still be visible on his head, side, back, hands and feet (John 20:25–27). There are frequent reminders that he shed his blood to redeem human beings of every type (5:9; 7:14; 12:11).

Yet the Jesus of Revelation is also very different from the man of Galilee. His first appearance to John was so awesome that this disciple who had been closest to him (John 21:20) fell in a dead faint. We have already mentioned his snow-white hair, blazing eyes, sharp tongue, shining face and burnished feet.

Though there are brief glimpses of the angry Jesus in the Gospels (Mark 3:5; 10:14; 11:15), his sustained 'wrath' in

Revelation strikes terror in the hearts of all kinds of people, who would rather be crushed by falling rocks than look into his eyes (6:16–17). This is no 'gentle Jesus, meek and mild'. Though that would be a doubtful description of him at any time, it is particularly inappropriate here.

Many believe Jesus preached and practised pacificism, despite his assertion to the contrary: 'Do not suppose that I have come to bring peace to the earth. I did not come to bring peace, but a sword' (Matthew 10:34; Luke 12:51). Of course, his words can be 'spiritualized', but it is far less easy to explain them away in Revelation, where the most natural understanding of the final conflict is physical.

Jesus rides down from heaven on a horse of war rather than a donkey of peace (Zechariah 9:9; Revelation 19:11; compare 6:2). His robe is 'dipped in blood' (19:13), but not his own. Though the only 'sword' he wields is his tongue, the effect of using it is to slaughter thousands of kings, generals and mighty men (both volunteering and conscripted), as once that same tongue dealt death to a fig-tree (Mark 11:20–21).

Jesus is clearly depicted here as a mass killer, the vultures cleaning up the mess afterwards! This graphic portrayal comes as a shock to respectable worshippers used to seeing him gazing benignly from stained-glass windows. It will be an even greater surprise to those who use the weeks of Advent in the Church calendar to present him in nativity plays as a helpless baby. He will never be that again.

Has Jesus changed? We know that old age mellows some but others become cantankerous and even malicious. Has this happened to him during the intervening centuries. God forbid!

It is not his character or personality that have changed, but his mission. His first visit was 'to seek and save what was lost' (Luke 19:10). He did not come 'into the world to condemn the world, but to save the world' (John 3:17). He came to give human beings the opportunity to be separated from their sins before all sin has to be destroyed. His second visit is for the opposite purpose – to destroy rather than to save, to punish sin rather than pardon it, 'to judge the quick [living] and the dead', as the Apostles' Creed and Nicene Creed put it.

It has become a cliché that Jesus 'loves the sinner but hates the sin'. The former was clearly seen in his first coming; the latter will be just as apparent at his second. Those who cling to their sins must face the consequences. At that time 'the Son of man will send out his angels and they will weed out of his kingdom everything that causes sin and all who do evil' (Matthew 10:41). This 'weeding' will be as thorough as it will be fair. But if it is to be totally fair, it must be applied to believers as well as unbelievers (as Paul clearly teaches in Romans 2:1–11, concluding that 'God does not show favouritism').

Once again, we need to remember that the Book of Revelation is addressed exclusively to 'born-again' believers. The descriptions of his fierce opposition to sinning are intended to induce a wholesome fear in 'saints' as an incentive to 'obey God's commandments and remain faithful to Jesus' (14:12).

It is all too easy for those who have experienced the grace of our Lord Jesus Christ, to forget that he will still be their Judge (2 Corinthians 5:10). Those who have known him as friend and brother (John 15:15; Hebrews 2:11) are apt to overlook his more challenging attributes. At the least, he is worthy of 'praise and honour and glory and power, for ever and ever' (5:13).

Of the 250 names and titles given to Jesus in Scripture, a considerable number are used in this book and some are unique to it, found nowhere else. He is the first and the last, the beginning and the end, the Alpha and the Omega. He is the ruler of God's creation. That is *his relation to our universe*. He was involved in its creation, is responsible for its continuation and will bring it to its consummation (John 1:3; Colossians 1:15–17; Hebrews 1:1–2).

He is the lion of the tribe of Judah, the root (and offspring) of David. That is *his relation to God's chosen people Israel*. He was, is and always will be, the Jewish Messiah.

He is holy and true, faithful and true, the faithful and true witness. He is the living one, who was dead and is alive for evermore, who holds the keys of death and Hades. That is *his relation to the Church*. They need to remember his passion for truth, which means for reality and integrity, as opposed to hypocrisy.

He is King of kings, and Lord of lords. He is the bright morning star, the one still shining when all others (pop and film stars included!) have disappeared. That is *his relation to the world*. One day his authority will be universally recognized.

So many of these titles are introduced with a formula familiar from the Gospel of John: 'I am'. This is not just a personal claim. The phrase sounds so much like the name by which God revealed himself that using it directly led to assassination attempts and ultimate execution for Jesus (John 8:58–59; Mark 14:62–63). That it was intended to indicate shared divinity and equality with God is confirmed in Revelation by Father and Son claiming exactly the same titles: for example, 'Alpha and Omega' (1:8 and 22:13).

The world is coming to an end, but that end is personal rather than impersonal. In fact, the end is a person. Jesus is the end.

To study Revelation primarily to discover *what* the world is coming to is to miss the point. The essential message is about *who* the world is coming to or, rather, who is coming to the world.

Christians are really the only ones who are longing for 'the end' to come, every generation hoping that this will happen during their lifetime. For them 'the end' is not an event, but a person. They are eagerly awaiting 'him', not 'it'.

The penultimate verse (22:20) contains a very personal summary of the whole book: 'He who testifies to these things says, "Yes, I am coming soon".' There can be only one response from those who have understood: 'Amen. Come, Lord Jesus.'

The rewards of study

We have already noted that Revelation is the only biblical book to carry both a blessing on those who read it and a curse on those who tamper with it (1:3; 22:18–19). By way of summary, we shall now list 10 benefits that result from mastering its message, all of which assist authentic Christian living.

1. The completion of the Bible

The student will begin to share God's knowledge of 'the end from the beginning' (Isaiah 46:10). The story is complete. The happy ending is revealed. The romance ends in the wedding and the real relationship begins. Without this, the Bible would be incomplete. It would have to be known as the 'Amputated Version'! The striking resemblances between the first and last pages of Holy Scripture (e.g. the tree of life) make sense of all that lies between.

2. A defence against heresy

So often the cults and sects, whose representatives come knocking at our doors, major on Revelation. Their apparent knowledge of it deeply impresses churchgoers who have never grasped it, largely through lack of teaching (and lack of teachers who know it). They are unable to challenge the interpretation offered, which can be quite bizarre. The only real defence is a superior knowledge.

3. An interpretation of history

A superficial awareness of current affairs can leave anyone baffled as to any discernible direction. Since future events cast their shadows before them, the student of Revelation will find an astonishing correspondence with world events, as they clearly head towards a world government and a world economy. Any preacher who systematically expounds the book is likely to be given many relevant newspaper cuttings by his hearers.

4. A ground for hope

Everything is going according to plan, God's plan. He is still on the throne, directing affairs towards the end, Jesus. Revelation assures us that good will triumph over evil, Christ will conquer Satan and the saints will one day rule the world. Our planet will be cleared of all pollution, physical and moral. Even the universe will be recycled. The hope of all this is 'an anchor for the soul' in the storms of life (Hebrews 6:19). Paganism, secularism and humanism only appear to gain ground. Their days are numbered.

5. A motive for evangelism

There is no clearer presentation of the alternative destinies placed before the human race – the new heaven and earth or the lake of fire, everlasting joy or everlasting torment. The opportunity to choose will not last indefinitely. The Day of Judgement must come, with every member of the human race accountable. But the day of salvation is still here: 'Whoever is thirsty, let him come; and whoever wishes, let him take the free gift of the water of life' (22:17). The invitation to 'Come!' is issued jointly by the 'Spirit and the bride [i.e. the Church]'.

6. A stimulus to worship

Revelation is full of worship, sung and shouted by many voices. There are 11 major songs, which have inspired many other hymns down the ages, from Handel's *Messiah* to the 'Battle Hymn of the Republic' ('Mine eyes have seen the glory of the coming of the Lord'). Worship is directed towards God and the Lamb, not the Spirit; and never to the angels. 'Therefore, with angels and archangels, we laud and magnify your holy name ...'

7. An antidote to worldliness

It is so easy to be 'earthly minded'. As William Wordsworth reminds us:

> *The world is too much with us, late and soon,*
> *getting and spending, we lay waste our powers,*
> *little we see in Nature that is ours.*

Revelation teaches us to think more about our eternal heavenly home than a temporary 'Ideal Home', more about our new resurrection body than our old ageing frame.

8. An incentive to Godliness

God's will for us is holiness here and happiness hereafter, not vice versa, as many would wish. Holiness is essential if we are going to survive present troubles, overcoming internal temptation and external persecution. Revelation shakes us out of slackness, complacency and indifference by reminding us that God is 'holy, holy, holy' (4:8) and that only 'holy' people will share in the first resurrection when Jesus returns (20:6). The whole book, but especially the seven letters at the beginning, confirms the principle that 'without holiness no-one will see the Lord' (Hebrews 12:14).

9. A preparation for persecution

This, of course, is the fundamental purpose for Revelation being written. Its message comes across loud and clear to Christians who are suffering for their faith, encouraging them to 'endure' and 'overcome', thus keeping their names in the book of life and their inheritance in the new creation. Jesus predicted universal hatred of his followers before the end (Matthew 24:9). So we all need to be prepared.

Reader, if this is not already happening in your country, it will certainly come. And so will Jesus, before whom cowards will be 'shamefully exposed' (16:15) and condemned to hell (22:8).

10. An understanding of Christ

With Revelation, the picture of our Lord and Saviour is completed. Without it, the portrait is unbalanced, even distorted. If the Gospels present him in his role as prophet and the Epistles cover his role as priest, Revelation clarifies his role as King, the King of kings and the Lord of lords. Here is the Christ the world has never seen, yet will one day see; the Christ the Christian sees now by faith and will one day meet in the flesh.

After studying Revelation, no one can ever be quite the same again. Yet its message can be forgotten. That is why its blessing is not just for those who read it, even aloud to others, but for those who 'keep' what is written. This means that we 'take it to heart' (1:3; New International Version) as well as mind, but also that we put it into practice. 'Do not merely listen to the word, and so deceive yourselves. Do what it says' (James 1:22).

APPENDIX

REVELATION 20 AND
THE MILLENNIUM

Sadly, this chapter has led to deep divisions among Christians. So different are the interpretations that there is an unwritten agreement not to discuss them for the sake of unity.

Readers may well have heard about the three major views – *a*millennial, *pre*millennial and *post*millennial – but there are other variations.

Some are inclined to treat the whole issue as academic, speculative and irrelevant (a friend of mine called it 'a pre-post-erous choice'!) and have coined a new label: panmillennial (the vague belief that everything will pan out all right in the end, whatever we think now).

But hope is as integral to the Christian life as faith and love. What we are sure will happen in the future profoundly affects our behaviour in the present. Our 'millennial' convictions influence our evangelism and our social action.

In particular, our hopes for *this* world are crucial. Will it only get worse or ever get better? Will Jesus' return to this planet have any beneficial effect or simply write it off? Is he coming to judge the nations or reign over them? And why is he bringing all departed Christians back here with him (1 Thessalonians 4:14)?

The Lord does not reveal the future to satisfy our curiosity or give us superior knowledge but so that we may prepare ourselves for our part in it. If we were convinced that we were going to share his reign over this world, we would behave rather more responsibly now.

We need to look at the passage itself, in its own context; then ask when and why such widely divergent interpretations of it have arisen; and finally make some evaluation and hopefully reach a conclusion.

The biblical exposition

Verses 1–10 of chapter 20 in Revelation are the focus of the whole debate. It is important to review what is stated clearly before attempting to draw inferences from the passage.

The most striking feature is the repeated phrase 'a thousand years' – six times, twice with the definite article '*the* thousand years'. The emphasis is unmistakable. Whether the figure is taken literally or metaphorically, it clearly means an extended period of time, as most commentators agree. It is an era, an epoch.

Surprisingly little information is given here about this whole time. Indeed, only three things are told us. One single event at the beginning, another at the end and a continuous situation in between. The opening and concluding happenings both concern Satan, while the state in between is about the saints.

The 'millennium' starts with the removal of the devil from the earthly scene altogether. A descending angel with a huge chain seizes, binds, throws, locks and seals him. The five verbs emphasize the complete helplessness of the devil, which is confirmed by the plain statement that his career of brilliant deception is over – though only for the duration of the millennium. He is not thrown into the lake of fire (yet!) but is securely imprisoned in the 'Pit' or 'Abyss', usually thought of as under the earth, out of reach of and out of touch with its living inhabitants.

This banishment of Satan, together with the previous consignment of his two henchmen, Antichrist and the False Prophet (the two 'beasts' of Revelation 13), to the 'lake of fire' (19:20), will leave the world without a government, in a political vacuum.

In the second part of this millennial vision, John sees 'thrones' (only plural here and in 4:4), occupied by those given authority to 'judge' (ie. settle disputes, maintain law and order, apply justice). Within this larger group he notices particularly those who were martyred for refusing to worship the Antichrist or be branded with his number (666). What an amazing reversal of their former situation!

Obviously, both this small group and the larger one of which they are part have come back from the dead. They have 'come to life' again to reign with Christ during the millennium. This is specifically described as a 'resurrection', a noun only used throughout scripture with reference to physical bodies. We know that those who belong to Christ are thus raised at his coming (1 Corinthians 15:23). They are 'blessed and holy' to be raised then and become royal priests in the millennium and will never again run the risk of being consigned to 'the second death' (the 'lake of fire', i.e. hell).

There is in this passage a very clear distinction between this 'first resurrection' of the saints and the resurrection of 'the rest' of the human race. The two events are separated by the entire 'millennium'. And the two resurrections have too entirely different objectives. One is to reign with Christ, the other is to be judged (20:12).

The third section of this vision takes us to the very end of the millennium – Satan removed (1–3), saints reigning (4–6), and Satan released (7–10). This is an astonishing development, easier to attribute to divine revelation than human imagination! Who would have guessed that the devil would be allowed back on earth for a second (and final) attempt to claim it as his kingdom! Yet he is able again to deceive multitudes into thinking he can give them liberty, and to enlist a vast army to march on 'the camp of God's people, the *city* he loves' (surely a reference to Jerusalem). The forces are labelled 'God and Magog' (from Ezekiel we know this refers to an attack on the restored throne of David) and this assault is therefore to be distinguished from Armageddon (19:19–21). There is no battle. The forces are destroyed by fire from heaven and the devil finally joins the Antichrist and the False Prophet in hell to be tormented for ever (the Greek phrase 'to the ages of the ages' cannot mean less).

No reason is given for allowing the devil to have his final fling after such a long period of a godly government and all its benefits. But it will serve to underline the truth that the rebellion of sin comes from within the heart and not from the environment and to justify the immediate division of the human race into two groups – those who want to live under the divine rule and those who don't. The 'millennium' leads straight into the final day of judgement when this final separation takes place.

Two questions remain to be answered and they are crucial to understanding why there is such controversy over this 'millennium'. They are:

WHERE does all this happen?
WHEN does all this happen?

'The revelation of Jesus Christ' recorded in this book, consisting of verbal ('I heard') and visual ('I saw') elements, alternates settings between heaven and earth, relating events in both. But changes of scene are clearly indicated (4:1; 12:13).

The entire passage from 19:11 to 20:11 is clearly set on earth. The King of kings rides out of an open heaven to 'strike down the nations' on earth; the battle against the forces of Antichrist and the False Prophet takes place on earth; the angel comes 'down out of heaven' to banish Satan from earth; the martyrs 'reign with Christ' who is now on earth; Satan finally gathers his 'Gog and Magog' forces 'from the four corners of the earth'; the earth finally 'flees from the presence of the one on the great white throne'.

It is perverse to avoid the conclusion that the 'millennium' takes place on earth. 'Heaven' is only mentioned when someone comes 'out of' there to come here. That answers the question: 'Where?'

The question 'When?' would have an equally clear answer had not God's word been divided into chapters in the Middle Ages. This arrangement may be convenient (together with verse numbers, a separate but uninspired development) but the division is sometimes in the wrong place, setting asunder what God had joined together. This is especially true here. The bishop who inserted '20' into the text was clearly not afraid of the curse on those who 'add anything to the words of' the prophecy of this book (22:18). Little did he realize what damage it would do, though it probably reflected his own view, as we shall see.

If the three chapters 19, 20 and 21 are read as one continuous revelation, as the Lord intended, the sequence of *seven* visions (from 'I saw' in 19:14 to 21:1) becomes clear. They reveal the final events of world history, in the order with which they follow each other (for example, 20:10 refers back to 19:20

as having already happened). Dividing the visions between three chapters has meant that they are rarely read, much less studied, together. The sequence is lost. The events can then be juggled into a quite different order – and have been.

Anyone reading through Revelation, without any pre-conditioning of their minds and without letting chapter divisions have any influence, would naturally assume that the 'millennium' *follows* the return of Christ and the battle of Armageddon and *precedes* the day of judgement and the new heaven and earth. That is the simple and plain meaning of the text.

So the passage appears to reveal a lengthy period of Christian government on this earth after Christ returns and raises his own from the dead but before he finally judges the world. Why don't all Christians believe this – and look forward to sharing in the transformation it will bring?

The historical interpretation

For the first five centuries the church apparently agreed on the above interpretation. Over a dozen of the 'Fathers', as early theologians are called, mention what Papias, bishop of Hieropolis, referred to as 'the corporeal (i.e. bodily) reign of Christ on the earth'. There is not a hint of any other view, much less any debate about it. They assumed that scripture was to be taken as it stood, on this as on other matters.

This position, seemingly universal in the early church, is better known as pre-millennial, because it holds that Jesus will return *before* (i.e. 'pre') the 'millennium' describes in Revelation 20.

All this was to change through a North African bishop called Augustine, who has had more influence on 'Western' theology, Catholic and Protestant, than anyone else. He began with pre-millennial views, but later allowed his Greek education (neo-Platonic) to change his thinking on this and many other aspects of Christian belief and behaviour.

The basic problem was that Greek thought, unlike the Hebrew mind in scripture, separated the spiritual and physical realms, tending to identify the former as holy and the latter as sinful. Sex, even within marriage, came under suspicion and clerical celibacy followed.

Inevitably, the bodily return of Jesus to reign over a physical earth became difficult to handle and there may have been a reaction to over-indulgent preaching of physical pleasures on the millennial earth. Suffice it to say that even the 'new' earth tended to disappear and Christians only looked forward to 'going to heaven'. Jesus' second coming was reduced to judging the 'quick and the dead' and destroying the earth (actually, Revelation 20 puts these in reverse order). The Council of Ephesus in AD 531 was so heavily influenced by this new approach that it condemned pre-millennialism as heresy, which has caused it to be under suspicion ever since!

What should we do with Revelation 20? It is still part of God's Word and we cannot afford to ignore it. The simple solution is to transfer the millennium from after to before Christ's return, to claim that chapter 20 comes before chapter 19 in history, even if it doesn't in scripture! Chapter 20 masks a 'recapitulation' of events leading up to the second coming. It belongs to church history in the present, not the future.

Strictly speaking, this shifted the church from a pre-millennial to a post-millennial position, because it holds that Jesus will return *after* (ie 'post') the 'millennium' described in Revelation 20!

But there was an ambiguity in all this, that was to lead to a further major division of views. Augustine did not spell out clearly whether this new 'millennium' was a purely *spiritual* reign of the saints with Christ (which in a sense could be applied to the whole church history, from the first to the second coming of Christ) or whether it would be *political* as well (when the church would have become strong enough to take over the government of the nations in the name of Christ). His book *The City of God*, written when the Roman empire was collapsing, does not make it clear whether he expected the 'Kingdom of God' to take over from Rome (which it virtually did) or merely survive and grow in spite of the catastrophe. This paved the way for two schools of thought, both claiming roots in Augustine.

On the one hand are those who believe the church will 'Christianize' the world, not by converting everyone but by gaining political power to apply God's laws – and thus introduce a lengthy period (even literally a thousand years) of universal peace and prosperity, incidentally relegating the second coming to the distant future, since this 'millennium' hasn't even started yet and, indeed, seems to be further off than ever. But this idea has often resurfaced – in Victorian missionary hymns coinciding with the expansion of a 'Christian' British Empire, for example; and more recently under labels like Restoration, Reconstruction and even Revival. This optimistic outlook has claimed exclusive use of the adjective 'post-millennial'.

On the other hand those who believe the 'reign' of Jesus and his saints is purely spiritual and began at the first advent and will continue to the second, have had to find a new title for themselves and have chosen 'a-millennial'. This is both inaccurate and misleading, since the prefix 'a-' means 'non' (as in 'a-theist'). It is still post-millennial in both believing the 'millennium' is a period of time before Christ return, but only differs from other 'post-millennials' in believing that we are *already* in the millennium and have been for two thousand years!

This view, going back through the Protestant Reformers to Augustine, is probably the most common view in Europe, though not in America, as we shall see. It is worth pausing to note how Revelation 20 is handled by those espousing it.

Many subtle changes have to be made. The 'angel' dealing with Satan becomes Jesus himself, the 'binding' taking place either at his temptations or crucifixion. Satan is bound but not banished. He is merely put on a long chain, so only limited in his movements (thrown, locked and sealed are dismissed as meaningless). Usually the 'limit' on his activities is solely an inability to prevent the gospel spreading and the church being built. He is left on earth, not shut up in a pit or 'abyss'. Those martyred under Antichrist represent all saints throughout the ages reigning in heaven with Jesus. Their 'coming to life' in the 'first resurrection' was either their conversion (raised from the 'death' of sin) or their going to heaven at their death – but nothing to do with their bodies. However, the 'rest' 'coming to life' (the same word in the same context) *does* mean raised bodies! And all six times, a 'thousand years' means at least two thousand so far.

And so it goes on. The reader's common sense is left to judge whether all this is good *ex*egesis (reading out of scripture what is clearly there) or bad *eis*egesis (reading into scripture what one wants to find there). This author finds such interpretation totally unconvincing.

There has been one other major development in the millennial which needs to be noted, not least because it is widely held on the other side of the Atlantic, though it originated over here, in the teaching of John Nelson Darby, founder of the Brethren movement. It was popularized by his pupil, an American lawyer called Dr C. I. Scofield, who produced the 'Scofield' Bible, and by a seminary in Dallas, Texas, especially through a former student, Hal Lindsay.

The positive side is that, from the early nineteenth century, many were led back to the pre-millennial conviction of the early church. It had never entirely disappeared (Isaac Newton was a supporter of this view) and others would rediscover it including Anglican bishops like Ryle, Westcott and Hort, but the major influence came through the Brethren.

The negative side is that Darby combined this ancient belief with some quite novel notions in a complete theological system now known as Dispensationalism, after the seven eras, or dispensations, into which he divided history, in each of which God dispensed his grace on a different basis. He taught that the church was in a state of irrecoverable ruin; that the Jews were God's 'earthly' and Christians his 'heavenly' people, kept separate for all eternity; and, above all, that Christ would come again *twice*, once secretly to take his church away before the Great Tribulation and then publicly, to rule the world. His detailed schedule of the future also included four separate judgements.

Tragically, all this was so tightly integrated that it is widely thought that a pre-millennial belief must be 'dispensational'. To reject the latter is to reject the former! But that is to throw away the baby with the bathwater (a saying dating from the days when a whole extended family used the same tin bath and by the turn of the youngest the water was so muddy that it's final occupant could be overlooked!).

It is therefore necessary to make a very clear distinction between the 'classical' pre-millennialism of the early church and the 'dispensational' premillennialism of many modern Evangelicals and Pentecostals. A small but growing number of biblical scholars are realizing this (the names of George Eldon Ladd and Merrill Tenney spring to mind).

A personal conclusion

I will close this Appendix with the reasons why I am a 'classic pre-millennialist' in interpreting Revelation 20.

1   It is the most natural interpretation, without any forcing of the text.
2   It gives the most satisfying explanation of why Jesus needs to come back and bring us with him.
3   It is the view that gives greatest emphasis to the hopeful expectancy of his return.
4   It explains why God would want to vindicate his Son in the eyes of the whole world.
5   It 'earths' our future, as does the whole New Testament, heaven being a waiting-room for us.
6   It is realistic, avoiding the post-optimist and the a-pessimism, as regards this world.
7   It has fewer problems than the other views, though it still leaves some questions unanswered.
8   It is what the early church unanimously believed and they were nearer to the apostles.

For these reasons, I am able to pray, with real meaning and longing: 'Your kingdom come on earth ... as it is in heaven'.

Note: This whole issue is dealt with in greater depth and detail in 'The Millennium Muddle', the fourth section of my book *When Jesus Returns* (Hodder and Stoughton, 1995).